EVERYTHING RUSTLES

To him who is in fear everything rustles.
—Sophocles

EVERYTHING RUSTLES

Jane Silcott

ANVIL PRESS • VANCOUVER • 2013

LIBRARY AND ARCHIVES CANADA CATALOGUING IN PUBLICATION

Silcott, Jane, 1956-
    Everything rustles / Jane Silcott.

ISBN 978-1-927380-41-3

    1. Silcott, Jane, 1956-.   2. Middle-aged women--Biography.   I. Title.

HQ1059.4.S54 2013   305.244'2092   C2013-901591-4

Cover design by Rayola Graphic
Interior design by HeimatHouse
Author photo by Daniel Henshaw

Anvil Press gratefully acknowledges the support of the Government of Canada through the Canada Book Fund, the Canada Council for the Arts, and the Province of British Columbia through the British Columbia Arts Council and the Book Publishing Tax Credit.

Anvil Press Publishers
P.O. Box 3008, Main Post Office
Vancouver, B.C. Canada
V6B 3X5
www.anvilpress.com

Printed and bound in Canada

For my parents

CONTENTS

PREFACE

I started writing this book years ago, long before I knew I was writing a book. I was just trying to find out what I thought about things. Some of these things were personal—motherhood and marriage, hugely intimate subjects. Others were small events out in the world, interactions with strangers that struck deep for some reason, so the outward became inward. Writing was difficult. I struggled. During dinner with two fabulous friends, one of them said, it's about the voice, finding the voice to speak through. She didn't say "speak through," though. She said something better, but I can't remember it now—memory is one of the things that's eroded with age, or perhaps melted. Dissolved, grown thin and pale and unreliable. That makes me think of the word "fey," a word I love, suggesting things that are otherworldly, things we need to listen closely to in order to hear.

As I was writing these pieces, and the pile of them grew, the inward, the outward, the mix between, I recognized I was writing about age an awful lot—the long look back, the shorter look forward—and that the only thing that gave me the courage to actually consider putting all this "I" out in the world was the inevitable end to the story. If I don't say what I want to say now, when will I?

That said, on the eve of releasing this book into the world, I am afraid. Some of these essays are so personal I wish the printer could use a special ink that recognizes any tie between me and the reader and could—like

Harry Potter's cloak of invisibility—just make it quietly disappear. Alternatively, if the publisher had let me, I would have prefaced some pieces here with a list of those dear to me, beginning, "Aunt Sheila, please don't read this."

The quote from Sophocles that gave me the title of the book is something I love to ponder. Fear makes everything rustle, yes. But so does life—and maybe love. Maybe fear feels bigger with age because so does love. The synonyms for "rustle" are susurration, sough, whisper. Beautiful words, all. I think of small animals in the brush, my family moving around the house, and even the cells of my skin drying out, rustling against one another, like feet moving through leaves.

ACKNOWLEDGEMENTS

This book wouldn't have been possible without friends and family whose intelligence, support and love feed my mind and my life. Bob, Colin, and Olivia Walker—my loves, best friends, and much valued readers and editors. My classmates, teachers, mentors from Banff, Vancouver, UBC, Langara: the lonely life of a writer is a misnomer with all of you in it. My siblings, Suzanne, Doug, and Mariah Hamilton—ever gracious about having a writer in their midst. The magazines that first published several of the essays in the book: *Geist*, *Eighteen Bridges*, *Room*, *Maisonneuve*, *subTerrain*. My friend, Ross Belot, who talked his daughter Erinn into running barefoot through leaves in October, then donated the gorgeous photos for the cover. The fine people at Anvil Press: Brian Kaufman and Karen Green whose support and faith throughout the process have been invaluable. And because Stephen King says, "to write is human, to edit is divine," my last thank you is for those who helped edit these pieces as we headed towards the publishing deadline: Luanne Armstrong, Fiona Tinwei Lam, Andrea MacPherson, and finally, the shimmering Mary Schendlinger, editor extraordinaire.

Thank you to the Canada Council for its invaluable financial support during the writing of this book.

The following essays have appeared in slightly different forms in the following publications: "Threshold" and "Everything Rustles" appeared in *Eighteen Bridges*. "Semantics" appeared in *Maisonneuve*. "Lurching Man," "Natty Man," "A Leap and a Blessing" (published as "Gangly Man"), "The Plot of a Life," "Ducks," and "Mimesis" appeared in *Geist*. "The Goddess of Light & Dark" appeared in *Room*, and "Hum" appeared in *subTerrain*. "Ghosts" was published in *Body Breakdowns: Tales of Illness and Recovery* (Anvil Press, 2007), and "Natty Man" was published in *Slice Me Some Truth* (Wolsak and Wynn, 2011). The author is grateful to the editors of all of these publications.

The quotation in "The Man Who Met Sontag" is from "Self-Hatred, The Right to a Life, and The Tasks of Mid-Life" by Sharon McQuaide, in *Clinical Social Work Journal*, Vol. 24, No. 1, Spring 1996.

THRESHOLDS

THE MAN WHO MET SONTAG

IT'S NOVEMBER. AN IMPOSSIBLE MONTH. Grey hangs over the city. "A brooding sky," the announcer says on the radio, and then plays an oboe concerto, which soars and hums and makes low throaty sounds, a defence against brooding. I go to a bookshop looking for Susan Sontag. I had come across the title *As Consciousness Is Harnessed to Flesh*, and thought, there's another mind I want to know. After browsing the shelves awhile, I ask the man behind the counter for help, then because of something in his face when I say "Sontag," or maybe just a general openness or look of familiarity, I add, "I feel like a failure because I haven't read her yet."

"Don't say that," he says right away, which is generous, seeing as he doesn't know me and can't possibly account for all the ways I've failed, but I know he's right. That sort of statement isn't helpful, not if you want to be a contributing member of society, useful and good instead of a faded wisp lying on the ground thinking of all the books you haven't read. So I laugh. Besides, I don't really mean it. What I am failing in at that moment is finding words. "I mean, a gap in my reading. A hole that needs to be filled," I amend.

"Ah," he says, nodding. "I don't have the one you're looking for, but I might have something here. I've read her earlier books. My girlfriend used to read her." I follow him to a shelf and we skim through together but don't find her. "She could be in my women's section too," he says after a minute, so we move a few feet away, while I ponder the sudden strangeness of "women's section," as if I've never heard it before, a separateness, a smaller, contained space. It could be because earlier in the day I'd also been thinking of the exclusive golf club my mother belonged to, where she had kept up my membership long after I'd moved away from home. There was a dress code there and sections for men where women couldn't go, and then sections for women where children couldn't go, and then, finally, a small section for children. The man looks and I look. Still no Sontag. "I need some Sontag," he says. "I'll get some."

I go home and read an article by Sharon McQuaide about middle age. Jung is in it and a woman with debilitating self-esteem issues. "If self hate persists, the self has the firmness of smoke," the article says. Lovely metaphor. I think of days when my self seems to be hiding behind a cloud (self as sun, self lighting the way)—or days like today, happy and thinking about words and other ephemera and how that whole idea of self is mysterious and sinuous and wavery and, yes, firm as smoke. The woman with no self-esteem recovered. She had lost sight of herself because her parents, for some twisted reason of their own, needed to believe she was weak and helpless. And so she had played that role to allow them to keep their ideas of themselves intact, ideas that must have been as brittle as scaffolds, as barriers and rules. I think about love, what we do for it and to ourselves. And I think about the golf club and its scaffolds and my mother.

And then I find out that the Sontag title I fell in love with is a collection of her writings edited by her son, which proves something else about love, I'm not sure what, but something.

The man in the bookstore told me he'd met Sontag at a dinner in Edmonton "a hundred years ago," and I smiled, recognizing a phrase I use more and more. "Sontag was amazing," he said. "I mean, I had to learn to eat with my jaw hanging open." He let his jaw drop for emphasis, an open hinge. I decided I liked him, and realized I'd seen him somewhere before, but don't remember where. Sometimes this getting older feels a little like joining a new club. I see fellow members everywhere, and I appreciate them for their lines, their greyness. There's a kind of ease in it, familiarity, and also relief. What's been barring me from this club all these years has just been youth, and now I'm here, careening towards age, hurtling on a downward slope, and when I see my fellow careeners, I feel reassured. I look at them and nod, and think, "Here we are. We might as well make the most of this little moment."

THRESHOLD

M Y HUSBAND IS A LIAR. When I complain about the wrinkles on my neck, he says, "What wrinkles?" Then I laugh because I don't want to press the point. Would it be a good idea to have him examine, truly, the decay that is my neck skin? Think wattle. Think chicken with pinfeathers that spring out overnight.

I care about these things now, but can imagine a future where I won't. When the dementia was first catching my mother, there were days when she might open a suitcase and put a hanger in it and then a shoe. A while later, when her mind clicked back again, she'd say, "It's terrible getting old. I don't know things anymore, and I get so upset." It was terrible seeing her in that phase. Later still when she didn't know me but would smile when I visited her in the home, it seemed better. But maybe it was just better for me.

In childbirth, there's a phase called transition. The cervix isn't quite fully dilated so it's not safe to push yet. The experts talk about this as a time when a woman may feel as if the walls are closing in, and then they talk of the pushing that comes after as though it will be a relief, and everyone in prenatal class nods and says, "Oh, good, pushing." And so begins another of those lies you buy into until you're in labour and realize that this "pushing" word is just another euphemism for agony.

Everyone yells encouragement at you when you're in childbirth as if you're in a race, and so you do the best you can, but you want to scream at them all to shut up so you can concentrate. But you can't scream, because something in your personality or your upbringing has bred you to be silent when stressed. Besides, you know if you start, you might never stop. You might become the screaming woman, the woman who goes into labour and stays there.

Chaos, disorder, mind-ripping pain. That was pushing. And that might have been transition. I don't know if I recognized the borders of either during the labours of my children, but I recognize them now—a feeling that the edges are closing in. Maybe that's what my mother felt, and the hanger and the shoe in the suitcase and the following around of the cat with the tin of food were all part of her trying to make the walls bigger, trying to make sense of them. I'm not sure. How can I ever know unless I follow her into Alzheimer's myself, and then what good will that be? None, except to find (as I do, the older I get) how much there was to admire in her, and how little I understood her when she was alive.

"We're giving birth to the next phase of our lives," a friend says over coffee—soy lattes, as it happens. The menopause experts would approve. We laugh, and then she tells me she feels like a teenager again, and I say that makes sense. Though what do I know? I'm menopausal myself, and sometimes can't remember where I am in a sentence. People say we forget things in midlife because we have too much information in our brains, and some of it has to be offloaded. I think it may be because I haven't had eight consecutive hours of sleep since 1991. But never mind. The mind is plastic, experts say—not the menopause or birthing experts, the brain experts, usually men. They note how other parts of the brain will step in and take over the job that an injured part can no longer accomplish. Maybe my mind is learning new skills too—like how to make do without the names for things, or my keys.

Physically menopause is the ending of a woman's periods, and scientists say the word actually only refers to the time when a woman's periods have been gone for a full year. Scientists call points like these "thresholds," which makes it sound simple (the same way that "transition" initially does). You imagine stepping over this threshold and moving from one state of biological being into another. And this sounds fine. Anyone can step. The body does it of its own accord, whether you want it to or not. Many of us step and then make a big hurrah out of it, as if we're celebrating. I even had a party, because it happened to coincide with my fiftieth birthday. At this party a friend gave me a book about women in their fifties who accomplish amazing things. Another friend gave me a papier mâché container shaped like an egg—and a significant look, which I ignored.

It's time to admit that the reason I started this essay is entirely superficial, which is embarrassing, but there we are. Some things, I hope, can be confessed and then dismissed. It began with a conversation with a man, an attractive man as it happens, but an academic conversation—the sort that can fire up in a hallway and spin out into the larger air so that everything seems to open up and new ideas rush in. We were talking about aging and then gender, and so for me, the obvious topic of menopause came up. And because this was one of those conversations where minds seem to spark one against the other in a higher, rarer air, I thought it was safe to mention something personal, so I said I was menopausal. It's not as if he jumped back or anything. He didn't run. But there was something. A squinching, if you can call it that. A momentary tightening in his pupil (only one, because you can't look at two at the same time, which seems wrong, but there it is—another limitation of the human body), and I felt suddenly and overwhelmingly ashamed. Why was that? Why be ashamed over a completely common experience? This man is a man's kind of man, all burly and hearty, but also sensitive and intelligent and so I admit I felt attracted. Or, more particularly, I felt a need to be attractive. But in that moment when his pupil squinched, I understood—perhaps for the first time—what the meaning of menopause really is.

In *The Change*, Germaine Greer describes menopause as "the begin-ning of the third age. The age when we are aware (finally) of our mortality, when time becomes precious and moves too quickly, when our looks change and we realize how much we'd relied on them most of our lives, when we lose power and identity (in Western cultures particularly), when we grieve for the loss of our fertility, and maybe also for the loss of libido. Our bodies are changing out from under us. It is the change that ends changes. It is the beginning of the long gradual change from body into soul."

This is beautiful. Safe at my desk, no mirror anywhere near, I imagine this graceful slide towards purity. I think of my father's skin as he aged, getting smoother and thinner, the folds on his hands like fine silk, under them the ripple of vein, everything coloured: tea-brown age spots, aubergine veins like the rivers on maps. But my middle-aged hands are more like my mother's, my right index finger an exact replica, the slight bend to the left, as if it's not sure of the way forward, the folds around my knuckles, which aren't thickening yet but tingle some days in anticipation of future immobility. The top of my back curves forward like hers did. My husband says it's because I look down all the time. He was following my mother and me in Toronto as we navigated a narrow, snowy sidewalk. "You and your mother, you never look up. What's with that?" I told him it was because we didn't want to slip, but I know it's also a dowager's hump and don't want to say those words to him: "dowager," "hump."

I know I'm failing on this passage. This journey towards soul. I'm stuck, not just groping for words, but stumbling around in endless circles of thought, and then into grief over looks, which is vain and silly and useless. I take some comfort in thinking that surely in this culture of plumpers and fillers and freezers, I'm not alone, and that some part of me may be excused for clinging to old vanities and habits. But the phrase "aging gracefully" haunts me, and I think I should hold myself to that higher ideal, forget my small vanities: my chicken neck, my disappearing eyebrows. Aim for a mindlift, instead of a facelift.

On the library shelves there are countless books on menopause, offering guidance and advice: cheering words about the benefits of giving up caffeine and red meat, taking up yoga and meditation. The women on the covers look competent and tidy, their hair neat, their faces remarkably unlined. Inside, they talk of menopause as if it's something we can manage, like a stock portfolio or a new diet. If we eat enough yams, take enough vitamins, begin each day with sun salutations and affirmations. In theory I'm all for health and responsible living, but in practice it turns out I'm the same person I was as a teenager: resentful, irresponsible, lazy, easily distracted.

In parts of South America and Africa, women are freed by menopause. In Botswana, for instance, the older !Kung women join the older !Kung men to tell stories and swear, to make lewd comments and smoke cigars. This sounds like a lot more fun than worrying about whether or not I look good or if I've achieved anything worthy in my life. In Western culture, one of the menopause books cheerfully tells me, middle-aged women free themselves from old patterns in their lives. They tell their husbands to do the dishes and they stop buying groceries and feeding the cat. They find new strength, shuck off old, inhibiting habits, and become more fiercely alive and productive than ever. As I passively wipe the counters in our kitchen one more time because it's easier than haranguing the teenagers into doing it, I think, yet again, I'm doing something wrong. I can't even get menopause right. I think of my mother on the beach at our family's summer gathering place with her sisters and cousins, all of them in their upholstered bathing suits, the kind with skirts and lots of pleating. Their hair fluffed out from their heads in clouds of grey or blue, or plastered flat under a fishing hat with hooks stuck into it (my mother). They all had bags of knitting beside them, and they seemed entirely content with themselves, their larger shapes, their wrinkled faces—all of it part of some big joke. Before dinner, they might have a large glass of gin, and after, they might gather again for another. As I head off to exercise class, drinking a glass of soy milk before I go, I think of girdles, cigarettes and gin. Why was I born into this relentlessly earnest time of herbal remedies and yoga classes? Why can't I take advantage of stimulants and supportive underwear?

My friends and I sit around my kitchen table lamenting our late starts in maternal life. The hard west light blasts in. None of us looks young in this light. We're wrinkling. The flesh is sinking. I have the beginning of jowls, one friend a series of cross-hatched lines on her forehead. We talk about surgery—what would it do for us?—and then we change the topic. We're home with teens. Trapped, it seems, by oversized toddlers who require our minds as punching bags, our spirits as invisible fences. Boundaries, the parenting books remind us. Limits. You're there to provide them. But what if I want to leap over those fences myself? What if I'd rather be running or dancing or singing through fields of flowers? (Oh stop, I tell myself. You'd strain a knee.)

On the internet, I find sad stories by men about their wives suddenly leaving them at fifty, riding off into the sunset on motorcycles, clinging to the leather jackets of unsuitable men, or wearing the jackets themselves— and here I picture them gleefully waving goodbye, responsibilities and the dinner dishes behind them.

On my bicycle one day a fellow cyclist gave me a hot-eyed stare while we were both stopped at an intersection. True, I'd been studying his calves, but innocently, I tell myself now—my admiration purely aesthetic for something round and well formed. I looked away but, as I followed him for the next few blocks, imagined a life where I didn't make dentist appointments and keep them, a life involving men who rode boldly into intersections, light bouncing off their calves.

Maybe the hormones are making small leaps, desperate last gasps at lust and liveliness as I stare down the haunting visions of old age: a friend's arthritic fingers in my mind's eye, another friend's chronic fatigue, another's brushes with cancer, another's missing lung, another gone, years gone. A tree she bought us as a sapling full grown in the yard, a photo, her business card in my drawer. Is this all we leave behind? No wonder we leap for men at intersections, small dreams of our former selves.

I know I'm also mentioning this encounter because I want to think there might still be something about me capable of attracting a strange man. How strange? I imagine a Harpo Marx type asking, but never mind. This isn't meant to be funny. It's more pathetic really, a woman seeing the end of her road of desirability. I wonder if the bicycle man was issuing an invitation at all. I could be deluded. My menopausal brain could be making up stories to ease me through. In *Dr. Susan Love's Menopause and Hormone Book*, Love calls menopause "adolescence in reverse" and says that estrogen is the "domesticating hormone" that turns premenstrual girls—confident, lively, engaged—into weedy romantic idiots. (The latter is my turn of phrase.) Menopause is actually a recovery stage, says Love, a stage where we return to our true selves. Who is that true self, I wonder, and does she do the dishes and care for her family, or does she go running off in search of fields of flowers—or in my case mountain cabins and night skies filled with stars?

Most of the menopause books begin with an explanation of the female reproductive cycle; several include a chart that shows four different-coloured lines to represent the four female hormones: estrogen, progesterone, luteinizing hormone (LH) and follicle-stimulating hormone (FSH). During the reproductive years, the lines follow a predictable series of ups and downs. In peri-menopause, the lines look like a two-year-old has gotten hold of the crayons—they shoot sideways across the page and then go straight up and cataclysmically down. At post-menopause everything goes flat. It looks like the lines on a heart monitor that you see on hospital shows when the music gets loud and the characters get silent. Maybe that's why not many books publish them. They're too harsh, too close a reminder of death. They make me think of the vistas of grief that open at unexpected moments: seeing the shape of a man like my father on the street, for instance, or thinking of my teenaged children, their faces turned towards the world, away from me. To let go of people first you have to let go of the part of yourself that needs them.

No one can tell me what happens to the individual cells when the hormones leave them. I'm not sure why I need to understand this, but it seems important to know what's happening deep inside my brain. What about those neurons that used to be flushed with estrogen at regular times every month? How do they cope? The medical people give me vague answers or strange looks. I search journals, the internet—nothing. Eventually I decide to think of my cells as little homes that have been visited by hormones for the past thirty-five years. Now the hormones don't come by anymore. They don't even call. I think of my cells drooping, looking for substitutes, sidling inappropriately up to other cells, or just lying in their little cell beds with the lights off and the blankets drawn up over their nuclei. I wonder how long this phase will last, this pause between infertility and acceptance. How long before I discover something to fill the gap, to spackle over the craters hormones have left behind, with knitting, say, or birdwatching? I visited an elderly cousin last summer. She's sinking into Alzheimer's, but when she said something about youth and slenderness, her sigh was full of consciousness. We laughed a sort of hopeless laugh together, the kind that's full of grief. Maybe the years and years of hormones have left traces behind, like tattoos. Maybe sometimes they burn.

Some women say just before ovulation they feel a spike of desire, and that even after menopause they have fluctuations in their hormones. Some time after the bike man incident, I sat on a small patio next to the pool where my daughter was having her swimming lessons. A young man entered. I recognized him from the day before, though it was a corner-of-the-eye recognition, and when I studied him more closely, I was a little surprised I hadn't taken greater note of him earlier. He was deeply tanned and muscled; his skin glistened with droplets of water from the pool. He asked if the chair beside me was taken, then moved it into the sun nearby when I said no. I kept writing, ignoring him, almost. He sat facing the sun, his feet up on the rail, his head resting on one hand, as if he was napping. I didn't look at him, though I thought he wanted me to. At least that was what I imagined, remembering what I was like at that age, self-conscious in almost everything. A while later when he asked the time, I answered him and walked away thinking that if I were younger I might have woven a fantasy out of that moment, a life, and a story. Then I was more intrigued by my lack of interest and how much I was looking forward to taking my daughter and her friend out for ice cream. I wanted to hear their thoughts, glean whatever bits of their minds they'd allow me to see.

"Only when a woman ceases the fretful struggle to be beautiful can she turn her gaze outward, find the beautiful and feed upon it. She can at last transcend the body that was what other people principally valued her for and be set free both from their expectations and her own capitulation to them." —Germaine Greer, *The Change*

.

Last summer I was sitting in a wicker chair on the screened-in porch of a rented cottage listening to the creek next to me and watching a wasp bump against the glass of the door. Cottonwood seeds drifted from the trees, looking like puffs of dust, slutswool floating through the air. The day before, as the sun was setting and I watched through the small frame of the kitchen window, the light had caught them so they looked like snowflakes against the green lawn and the wood behind it, as if someone had made a snow globe and set it with grass and trees. So that next day I was still fascinated, still thinking of them as floating feathers or fairy dust, something incongruous and magical, something to be watched—care-fully—and as I sat there I felt all the other moments when I'd felt the soft air of summer all around me and had time to look and listen, and so I was happy, really truly at peace with myself and everything around me, and I'd been writing about love and desire, which also made me happy, but the fluff caught my eye and that was more important.

Every day I unlearn. Today I read Germaine Greer again and am inspired. To let go of beauty is to find beauty. Yes. True beauty is outside us; we find it when we turn our minds away from ourselves. Yes. And isn't that a relief, to no longer consider oneself as if on a market shelf? To age gracefully is to say it doesn't matter if you become invisible in the world, and it doesn't matter if no man except your husband (who is bound by habit and good manners to do so) says you are beautiful. It doesn't matter. During childbirth, people cheer you on through the transition. No one cheers you on through menopause. You are meant to do it privately in the quiet of your room. I imagine the voices telling me to do so now (you can't write that! you can't say that!). But why be quiet about a birth? Besides, our bodies announce themselves. People used to call hot flashes "blooms." How apt. We flushing, heated women blooming out everywhere.

THE GODDESS OF
LIGHT & DARK

T HE INSIDE OF MY vagina is pink and rich with flesh. It isn't the
smooth tunnel I had imagined at all, but more of a cave with walls
that billow and move; they concertina in. At the end of it the cervix shines
pale pink, in its centre a small black hole that looks like a star imploding.
That's the os, the opening where babies and blood used to pass through.
"There it is!" the student nurse whoops. "We found it!" She and I give
each other the high five, as if we've just discovered the Holy Grail.

I'm in a health clinic at BC Women's Hospital looking at my insides
with the aid of a mirror and a light similar to the ones spelunkers use. It's
my first day as a clinical teaching associate. I am to be both model and
guide to nurses, midwives and naturopaths as they learn how to do pelvic
exams. I'm here because I need the work but also because my friend
Sandy, a nurse, has been telling me about the job for years. In other words,
I've had time to get used to the idea. Still, with my legs spread in front of
strangers, I feel as if I've joined a high-wire act—on top of the wire, the
clear air of women's health; underneath, embarrassment woven through
with a soupçon of shame. The student nurse whoops again. "That's
amazing," she says. "Aren't you excited?" I am, but not in any way you
might imagine because no matter how respectfully it's done, a speculum
up your hoo-ha is just not a good feeling.

The next student struggles to find my cervix, so someone calls for Lenore, the nurse practitioner in charge of the clinic today. I can't imagine anyone who wouldn't like her immediately. She has one of those honey voices that make you feel lucky to be hearing it and a way of looking you in the eye that makes you want to stand up straighter and be a better person, or at least be smart enough to keep up.

She pulls up a stool and looks me in the eye. "Is this okay?" she asks. I nod. Around a woman who's seen as many vaginas as Lenore has, there's no point in being embarrassed. Besides, I tell myself, with my body as blackboard, so to speak, there isn't much for me to do but lie back and think of England. The students gather close: a bouquet of heads staring between my legs—brown, black, blonde, like so many curious bees.

"Watch for the colour change," Lenore says. "See? There it is. Jane's cervix is posterior and a little to her right. Because she's post-menopausal it's flatter. In a pre-menopausal woman you'll see it rounder and more lush looking."

I don't mind this, really. My nurse friends have inured me to this sort of talk: "You should see the vaginas I see," my friend Sandy announced one day. "We're going to end up with labia hanging down to our knees and everything inside dried up like an old prune."

"God," I said, and then changed the subject, the better to absorb the idea of dragging genitalia. Funny the relationships we have with our body parts: love, hate, despair, ignorance.

The next four exams proceed with varying degrees of success. Whether the students find my cervix easily or not, they all seemed thrilled to be practising on a live, wide-awake woman. Later I find out why. Apparently doctors used to do their first "pelvics" on plastic models or cadavers. Then they hired prostitutes, and then nurses with half their bodies hidden behind sheets. Then someone came up with the idea of practising on women who were unconscious in surgery. I thought this was just another piece of dark medical history until I learned that the questionable practice is alive and well in some of Canada's teaching hospitals today.

In her book *Public Privates: Performing Gynecology From Both Ends of the Speculum*, Terry Kapsalis analyzes the cultural attitudes revealed in these practices and discusses the reasons behind all the subterfuge. She says doctors are afraid of many things, including hurting patients, appearing inept or disturbing the doctor-patient relationship. It's good to hear that doctors are afraid. It's humanizing and sort of endearing, and makes me think that it must take a certain amount of nerve and panache to touch strangers in intimate places.

When I'm done my work, I wait in the clinic lobby for Sandy. The student who whooped at discovering my cervix sits beside me. "Look!" she says. "Here's you!" For one surreal moment, I imagine she's taken a picture somehow, and I am just as excited as she is. I'm going to see my os on a page. But she opens a textbook to an illustration of the female anatomy. "There's your uterus, see? And there they are—the ovaries."

"Right," I smile, hiding my momentary disappointment. I'm still happy, but it's not something I know how to articulate. Later on, I'll read about women who describe the cervix as the most holy place in their bodies. At this point, I'm not too sure about the word "holy," but I do feel different. As I walk home, I have a new sense of myself. I am walking in the world, but I am the world too.

In early agricultural civilizations along the Nile, people worshipped a female figure whose body was the earth. She looked like a globe with legs and a head or maybe an orange on sticks, the kind of picture my daughter might have drawn in preschool. No Barbies there.

It's not that I feel like a globe exactly, but maybe seeing my cervix and os has plugged me in to a new power source. In her foreword to

The Vagina Monologues (the groundbreaking play by Eve Ensler), Gloria Steinem describes several examples of religious imagery that involve both male and female sex organs. Even more strikingly, Steinem describes material she discovered in the Library of Congress that says the basic layout of the Christian church is modelled on the interior of a woman's body: the outer doors represent the labia majora, the inner doors the labia minora, the aisle the vagina and the altar the womb. All this makes sense to me. Why not, if we're going to consider spiritual mysteries, begin with the mystery within our own bodies?

In the demonstration at the beginning of the clinical training days, one of the senior CTAs leads the session and Lenore stands back. There's purpose in this. "I want the students to recognize that the CTAs are, for lack of a better word, the 'power' in the place on that day," she says.

The students, usually ten or fifteen of them, line up against the back wall behind the instructor, whose name, like my friend's, happens to be Sandy— only this Sandy spells hers with an *i*. Sandi was one of the first CTAs in the program. Like Lenore, she projects an air of far-seeing intelligence. "When you first meet the patient, shake her hand and introduce yourself," Sandi begins, "that's your first neutral touch. Later, when she's sitting on the table with the sheet over her legs, tell her about the exam. Show her the speculum and mirror and explain what you'll be doing. Your second neutral touch is when you help guide the woman's feet into the footrests."

"Footrests, not stirrups?" someone asks.

"Yes. We're not riding horses here," Lenore comments, and everyone laughs. "Sorry, Sandi," Lenore adds. "I'll keep quiet now." Sandi continues, unflustered. She and Lenore and the long-term CTAs (several of whom are lay midwives) remind me that through the past fifteen years of childrearing, I've let my feminism get dusty. I'm a little afraid of all of them. What if they find out how bone ignorant I am? I see in these women that the business of the womb and the feminine can come as near to a vocation as you can get. They make me think of goddesses and female saints. You can go a long way on this journey. On the internet I find a site that sells vulva-shaped pillows and learn that the heart symbol we see on greeting cards was originally a representation of the vulva. Recently when my family and I stayed in a motel room festooned with hearts—on picture frames, towels, soap—it was a relief to think we were surrounded by the powerful vulva, rather than cheap sentiment.

"Buy a chocolate vagina!" a woman calls. She's standing on top of the steps to the student building at UBC. "Support V-Day. End violence against women and girls! Buy one. Only two dollars!" The woman is young and perky and holds the red-ribboned vaginas in her hand like a bouquet. "Do you want one?" she says. "Sure," I answer, feeling like we're sharing a joke, or a stance. Maybe a revolution. She directs me to the table where I can buy tickets to the play (*The Vagina Monologues* is performed annually as part of the V-Day campaign). After I pay, I take the vagina and unwrap it carefully. It's well formed. The inner lips flare, then tuck in like the petals of a flower. I'm hungry, but self conscious. Do I lick it or bite? Cowardly, I tuck it into my pocket and don't unwrap it until I'm near home. As I walk past a house near mine, licking, I hear a low guttural sound and am about to say "Shh" (expecting a dog) when an old man with a downturned mouth and grizzled cheeks steps into view. His eyes flick over me and he horks. The sputum hits the ground with a splat. A flush of disgust and anger rises in me; under it, a tiny thread of fear. The chocolate feels too soft in my mouth suddenly, my thoughts too fuzzy-edged. As I walk on, I think of all the people who would say, "You can't lick that! You can't write that!"

Onstage at UBC, student actors perform the monologues with gusto and grace. The stories range from funny to horrific to wonderful: from gyrations on a floor to war-sanctioned rape to raucously simulated orgasmic joy. In one of them a woman talks of a lover who just stared at her vulva without touching her. At first she was in an agony of embarrassment, but as he continued to admire her, she began to love what she'd always thought was shameful.

When I ask Lenore why so many women are uncomfortable with their genitals, she says it's a matter of exposure. "Men see their penises and others' penises, in gyms and washrooms, all the time. Women don't. We're not that bendy. We don't teach our women, our girls, to look at their vulvas. The only place you see vulva is porn, and what you see in porn is an idealized, sometimes surgically altered phenomenon."

The woman-centred pelvic exam begins with an observation of the external genitalia. Sandi teaches the students to offer a mirror to the patient and to say "Everything looks healthy and normal," rather than "nice" or "good." In the clinics, the protocol of the exam is as fundamental as the medical skills needed to gather cells for testing. When Sandi demonstrates the use of the speculum, the students ask questions about hand position and angle; they appear to fall on these technical details with some relief.

I sympathize. I know the first time I saw another woman's vagina I felt a little shaken. Maybe it's the interior flesh. It's so intimate and delicate looking—so frankly designed for sex. It seemed none of my business to look at another woman's parts; then too, there was the memory of my daughter's birth. Someone positioned a mirror so I could see. I was stunned. That angry, dark-looking beast was part of me? There's a picture of a screaming ostrich that reminds me of the vagina giving birth—all hair and redness and teeth—yes, teeth. I think that vagina/ostrich is saying, "Everyone, get the fuck out of my way. I'm working here."

The students come out of the demo room with a deer-in-headlights look. The biggest fear they'll acknowledge is that they might hurt me. It doesn't help that the speculum is shaped like a gun and the parts that open up inside the woman's body—now called "leaves" or "bills"—used to be called "blades." Another bit of language lore: "vagina" means "sheath for a sword."

The cervix is the tunnel end of the uterus. It extends an inch or so into the vagina like a turtle's neck. There's a bit of space on either side of it called the fornix. (I think of it as a place for sperm who forget to ask for directions.) Because my cervix is a little off to one side and posterior, some students have trouble finding it. I try to help, but that often makes it worse, and I wish I knew the coordinates and could say: "Two degrees east, four degrees south, proceed at a 33.5-degree angle. There. You've got it."

Once the student finds the cervix, she (usually a she) opens the speculum. The cervix moves into the space of its own accord and sits there like a cherry tomato in salad tongs. In a real Pap test, the next step would be to gently scrape the surface with a wooden spatula and then use a brush to collect more cells from inside the os, but students just simulate this part of the exam to avoid touching the delicate organ.

Created in the thirties, Pap tests are credited with having reduced cervical cancer rates throughout the developed world. "It's a brilliant, brilliant system," says Lenore. "This is an entirely treatable cancer if it's caught early enough." But even though it's a simple test, there are still women who don't have it. Aside from personal reasons, many women simply don't have easy access to a doctor, explains Lenore. "If you've got two little kids and a stroller and you've got to get on the bus, or if you live in an outlying region, and the doctor comes in once a month, and he (usually still a he) is still ten miles away down a dirt road and you don't have a car, it's an issue. Also, for aboriginal women there's a history of being treated really badly by the health profession."

Another reason women don't come in for Pap tests is that they don't see cervical cancer as a threat, says Lenore. "We don't know women who've died of cervical cancer in our age group. Our mothers did. Think about this . . . How did they sell women on having a speculum exam in the first place? They sold them because they knew women who had died of it. And cervical cancer is the worst way to die. Honestly, it's horrible. Basically you rot from the inside. It travels up and out. It's not fast. It's not pretty. It's smelly, and incredibly painful." When Lenore worked with cervical cancer patients twenty years ago the women were in isolation, with rods inserted in their vaginas to transport caesium, a radioactive substance, inside, and they had to be turned, like on a spit. "We really gave them tons of drugs," Lenore says. "It was pretty foggy for them, but still very uncomfortable." Nowadays, she says, the caesium is inserted via little "seeds," so there's no isolation and no spit to turn on, but the vagina can still be permanently scarred from the radiation burns.

Occasionally a nurse has said to me after the exam was over, "I couldn't do what you're doing." I nod and say, "It's not that big a deal," or, "I've gotten used to it." I don't say "Why not?" because I don't want to hear about how embarrassed they'd be to have strangers see their private parts. That might remind me that I could be embarrassed too, and while I've acquired a bit of confidence over the years and believe in the value of this work, I'm also aware how tenuous that confidence is, how easily it can tip over into doubt. In *Public Privates*, Kapsalis quotes a doctor who says, "My first question, as I suspect yours may be, was, 'What kind of woman lets four or five novice medical students examine her?'"

What kind of woman indeed?

When I ask a fellow CTA how she deals with the personal aspect of the work, she tells me something so brilliant and simple that I wonder why I don't have it tattooed into my brain. "I think of the students, not myself," she says, then explains further: "When I'm training people to do this work, I tell them to think of this half (she holds one hand at her waist, palm up) as the teacher and to think of this half (she turns her palm down) as the tool." This is excellent advice, but of course, with "tool," off my mind goes, and I have to resist making a bad joke. We don't know each other that well yet. After I thank her and say goodbye, I think of words, the trails they leave behind, the weight and heft of them in minds.

Every session Lenore holds, she and my friend Sandy sit in the hall outside the private rooms where we CTAs teach. They provide equipment and answer questions, but their primary job is to offer counsel and solace. "The thing with this training is that it's very emotional," says Lenore. "I always end up with one student in tears. Even if they're not outright sobbing, there's a lot that come out choked because this is something that's been traumatic for them. They've seen such roughness in medicine, and you remember, if you just look at stats, one in four women have been sexually abused, so it can be triggering."

Until recently, I had no idea what medical "roughness" meant, so when a student, trembling, told me she'd had a bad pelvic exam, I didn't fully appreciate why she was so upset. More fool me. Soon after, I had an exam with a doctor I didn't know. She came highly recommended, but it happened that she was using a plastic speculum for the first time. She found my cervix quickly enough, but when it came time to remove the instrument, instead of clicking it open to release my cervix as she should have done, she just pulled. "Ow," I said, "Ow!" and then "*Ow!*" until she stopped. When she finally opened the speculum, she jammed it wide, so the leaves (at that point feeling not far from their original moniker, "blades") pressed hard against the walls of my vagina all the way out.

That night I took three Tylenols and two Advils. I got in bed and curled into a fetal position and cried.

I like to think the extremes—failure/success—eventually balance each other out. But does this matter? I was hurt and deeply shaken. Others have been hurt far more seriously than I. One woman told me she'd had her labia torn by a doctor, another that her cervix was pulled right outside her body. "There's such roughness in medicine," Lenore repeats when I tell her, and she doesn't mean just physical roughness. Some women have been lectured or asked personal questions while the doctor's hand was inside of them.

I've been doing this work for two years now. I have seen my os many times. I know there's another os at the other end of the cervical canal that opens into the uterus. I like knowing this. I also like thinking about language and how the word "os" is Latin for mouth or opening, and it's also the root of the word for bones. For something to ossify means for it to become bone-like. The fact that there can be the same root word for a mouth and a bone makes me think the people who first named these essential parts of our architecture might have been more aware of their common purpose than of their differences. It also makes me think of caves again and the deep inner secret we women have inside of us.

I don't feel that same sense of awe and gratitude when I see my os anymore. With repetition, it's become a more ordinary sight, less the Holy Grail and more just another body part. Maybe that's fine. Maybe revolutions are about knowledge. And maybe confidence comes from thinking about all these mouths together: opening, closing, declaiming, objecting, singing.

HUM

For B.

EVERY ONCE IN A WHILE, I go to Banff to work. It's a place to get outside of myself, to be struck dumb by wonder. On the last morning of a recent trip there, I got up early and went for a walk. As I stood on a small slope watching the clouds settle around Mount Rundle like a blanket, something moved on the road below me. It was large and four-legged, a grey shape with a curving tail—a wolf? After I watched it trot several paces along the road then slip into the forest, I walked back the way I'd come. I was thinking of Russian novels and fear and Omar Sharif, in that order, and then, because it was morning, of coffee, and perhaps because of the grandness of the animal and the surrounding mountains, I chose a restaurant that was outside of my usually modest needs. I entered through carved wooden doors into a room with upholstered chairs and large, wood-mullioned windows. The room looked lived in, but cared for: the kind of place that makes me feel expansive and at the same time slightly unworthy. I had been standing there a few moments when a man in neat black pants and a white shirt approached me. His hair was grey at the temples, and he had fine wrinkles around his dark eyes and two narrow lines next to his mouth. "Are you all right?" he asked me. I couldn't answer at first for wondering if it was an existential question or if I should tell him about the wolf. It was still early, and I was in that state where things aren't quite certain. Maybe it hadn't really been a wolf. Maybe he wasn't really a waiter. I asked would it be all right if I had just a coffee, and he said, "Of course," and pointed to the newspapers on a table nearby. "Help yourself," he said.

The man never smiled, and we didn't speak more than a few words, but he appeared at my side every time my small cup was nearly empty, so I began to think of him as a person tuned to my thoughts. It could be I was simply enjoying having an attractive man serve me, or it could be that there was something in the quality of his attention that was true and real. Whatever it was, I became aware of the man, and then of desire and the way it can appear out of nowhere, then settle in, like a small song or a person humming.

The hum lasted all the way back to my hotel and made it into my notebook, and then it ended. While it was there, I felt buoyant. I felt things were possible that otherwise would be impossible, and I felt lighter and clearer and happier all round. My ideas about family and work were all still in their cherished places in my mind—I wasn't dreaming of running off with the man with the fine eyes and the lines by his mouth—not exactly. But the idea of it made me feel new again, remade.

I don't know if it's possible to determine where or why a hum begins. Perhaps there's a level of recognition that goes beyond the surface construction of self. Maybe I didn't have my outside self on yet that morning. The wolf may have shaken it loose. Then too, the man had asked me if I was all right in a way my husband might have, with a familiar note in his voice and his head tilted to one side as if to get a clearer view of me.

Some years ago I took part in group therapy. There were several bits of homework assigned. One was to stare into a partner's eyes for an extended period of time without talking. The therapists paired us up, and we did this first with the opposite gender, and then with the same. In both instances we acted as if it was a staring contest and made Ha-ha-isn't-this-silly faces at one another. But with silence you can't carry that off very long, and soon the nakedness of it feels shocking and strange. Each time there were tears, empathy, recovery, a period of reasonably comfortable "conversation" and then out of nowhere, unimagined and unlooked for, desire would appear. The fierceness of it and its reliable and startling presence was disturbing to all of us. It happened in each of the pairings, whether people were of the same sexual orientation or not. The worst was not being able to look away, having to negotiate an "Oh god I'm so sorry I don't really want that and I'm sure you don't either" sort of conversation without saying a word. It was excruciating and delicate and strange, and by the end of it we all agreed that if we went about staring into other people's eyes for any length of time without talking, we'd want to have sex with just about the whole world. But that wasn't the point. According to our deeply twisted therapists (not really, but definitely they had me wondering at times. You want me to do what?), the idea was to teach us about our common responses to intimacy, to learn that we could survive them, even fall in love a little, but still have our lives.

Brain cells communicate by shooting chemicals and electricity into the synapse between them. The communicating arm of a cell, called the axon, looks like a tail. The chemicals that are propelled through this tail by electrical pulses are picked up by small nubbins called dendritic boutons on the next cell. It's not exactly intercourse—not exactly like the spawning of salmon with the females laying their unfertilized eggs and the males spreading clouds of sperm over them—but it does sound pretty sexual: ideas spraying through our minds like ejaculate. Which makes me wonder: are we like cells walking around, and is the membrane of our skull a sufficient barrier, or are some electrochemical messages so powerful they spill out into the air?

One time at a speaking event with friends, we were all standing at the edge of the crowd. It was dark, the speaker was riveting, our minds leaned towards his next word. I knew who was behind me. I could feel him there. Not touching. But the space between us, the synapse, was charged. After, he smiled and put his arm around me, gave my shoulders a friendly squeeze, and we returned to our neutral friendship and our partners.

A while ago, the paid hands of a massage therapist drew sighs from me. I lay on the table, half naked, my back exposed to air, his hands pressing on me. No need for words, no need for me to do anything but receive his touch. "Breathe evenly," he had instructed me at the beginning of the session. "Same length of breath in as breath out." Fifteen minutes in, and I was putty. Naked putty, my breasts pressed into the warm sheet beneath me. Near the end, he held the covering sheet up like a tent and stood back. "Roll over," he said. Then he placed the sheet over me and used his fingers on my clavicles, the tops of my shoulders, the spaces between my upper ribs. My body fell away. I was the places he touched, no more.

"You're all talk," my husband complains. It's true. I am. But talk's good, isn't it? I love talk. I love the way words slide in, stir cilia, drop like small stones in the brain and set off ripples there. Years ago I was working as a sort of secretary, "sort of" because I wasn't very good at it. Every once in a while there'd be a voice on the phone that would set off an answering hum in my body. It was just sound, not anything the voice was saying, but I would have to be careful not to drop my own voice to match it, not to speak back with my vowels dripping.

When we have orgasms, our minds are flooded with dopamine. Well named. Dope. It's the happy hormone. The chemical of fireworks and fluffy clouds with bright shimmery outlines. We all love dopamine. If we could shoot up with it and not kill ourselves with happiness, we would. But we can't. Researchers have tried it with rats. They died (the rats, not the researchers), looking ragged, knocked thin and worn by surfeits of pleasure.

While searching for more information about hormones and sex, I come across a website proclaiming that we'd all live happier, more harmonic lives without orgasm. The writer argues that the hormones that follow the flush of dopamine—oxytocin and prolactin—are designed more to encourage breeding than connection with a lover, and that although oxytocin is sometimes described as the "cuddle" hormone, it's there during sex more for mechanical than emotional reasons. Oxytocin makes the uterus contract, creating little sucking waves that pull sperm in. Prolactin is the antidote to dopamine; it's the hormone that stops us from being sex addicts, apparently, and is at its base the thing that makes us get up, get dressed, and go out the door, thinking of the next person we can spread the seed with—or take it in. I find several more writings on the subject of no-orgasm sex—an article in the *Huffington Post* among them. They all have slightly different interpretations, but the general consensus is that the explosion of dopamine and the ensuing flush of the downer prolactin can be disruptive to relationships. The advice is that it's better to encourage quieter, more controlled intimacies that build oxytocin levels rather than dopamine explosions. There's much good in what they say. Who would argue against greater intimacy? I tell my husband about it, and we discuss fireworks and brain bombs, then agree that our vote is for both: intimacy and risk; even so, the no-orgasm article stays in my mind, and the next time, post lovemaking, I'm on alert for prolactin effects. We're out in the garden, cleaning up before a trip to a local manure sale. He says something innocuous but typical about the shrubs at the north end of the vegetable garden. They shade his plants, he says. "No they don't," I reply. "How can they?" It's an old argument, not important, but the feeling that wells up in me is so strong I wonder what I was thinking to marry him. At the manure sale, young men haul the bags for us. One of them mistakes another man for my husband and veers towards his car instead of ours. The man is about the right age, but his beard is neatly trimmed, his shirt tucked in, and he has spread tarps, clean and new looking, over the seat and floor of his van. I imagine briefly that the man is my partner, and that my life would be so guided and clean, and I know immediately I would be even more irritated with him than I am with my husband.

Electricity is everywhere. We are electrons with legs. We feel each other through air, click together or are repelled. At a party recently, I was talking to a group of women. The room was crowded. I looked across it and saw my husband talking to a woman I didn't know. They were at the edge of the crowd, his head bent just slightly towards hers. Something about the angle of his head and their separateness made me look again. We don't have a jealous marriage. We are secure in one another. Thankfully. Gratefully, secure. So this feeling of my husband's attention flaring towards someone else was rare. I'm not writing this because it bothered me. I'm writing it because he was fifteen feet away from me, twenty other minds were shooting their own electrochemical stews into the air between us, but I knew. I could feel the lean of his mind towards hers. Later that night, he told me about her, how quickly they'd connected, talking about riding their bikes to work, and then, without thinking how it sounded or what he was saying, he sighed, "I could have talked to her all night."

Buddhism says we are one, all of us connected—as if part of some giant organism, I wonder? During those moments when we recognize someone like ourselves, is it as if we're seeing a fellow body part? "Ah, there's another pancreas. I knew it right off, pumping insulin like nobody's business." Oneness. I feel it with women too. That rare and instantaneous recognition. What is it we see?

My aging friends and I sometimes sigh over the loss of our youth, of being attractive just for being young and female. We watch men walk past, then joke about our easy hearts, which sway and lean, following the good hard scent of them, the beauty of their muscled legs and easy laughs, the dark notes in their voices and the potential flare of sex in their eyes.

"We're sluts," we say, then laugh and change the topic. What else can we do? We're not likely to be welcomed by these objects of our desire. Our casualness is defensive, or possibly rational. The good thing about age is that eventually you learn that heat will pass, that it doesn't always have to scorch you the way it did when you were younger, when every flare felt like a direction signal, like you were a plane lost in the night, getting low on gas and desperately searching for a place to land.

The psychologist Jacques Lacan said desire is about emptiness. To have desire, first you have to have emptiness. We don't see the objects of our desire as beings (or things) separate and whole unto themselves, but as projections of our own yearning. This makes sense. After twenty years together, my husband is steady, a flame that can be both pilot light and conflagration. He tells me that my theory about the woman at the party is misconstrued. "That's fine. I don't mind if you put it in your essay, but you've got it all wrong." He's smiling at me.

I smile back. "No, I don't. You liked her."

"Yes, I liked her, but only because she was someone I could talk to at the party. I don't like parties where I don't know anyone. She didn't know anyone either."

I laugh, thinking how much fun it is to discuss moments of errant flame.

The other day our cat had a seizure. She's nineteen. I inherited her as a kitten from the same therapists who had given me the staring homework years ago. I heard a clattering sound in the bathroom and found her there on the heat vent, her legs jerking out in spasms, her claws rattling the metal flanges. As her body convulsed and moans issued from deep in her throat, I patted her head and spoke to her gently. My husband and daughter watched from over my shoulder. I felt their sympathy aligning with mine, all of us pouring love towards our cat. Finally the convulsions stopped, and she lay there looking as if she was broken in the middle, her hind end immobilized. Seizures are electrical misfirings in the brain, like lightning. Objects struck by lightning can catch fire or show no signs of burning at all. The cat recovered, pulled herself up from the floor, stumbled and yowled, until I held her in my arms. When I first met my husband I didn't really see the potential. It took a year, and then I couldn't look at him sometimes, for fear I might burn right there on the spot.

The wolf had trotted along the edge of the highway for less than a minute, moving in a straight line before something—a thought, a memory or a smell—had drawn it down the slope into the forest. It had looked so certain. Is that what I found so appealing? Or was it the wildness of it, the palpable sense of "other"? The man in the restaurant wasn't wild exactly, but he was an "other" with sparks and a sense of mystery in his eyes. I wasn't close enough to the wolf to look into its eyes, thankfully, but I know if I had been, before the fear struck, there would have been a moment of—not desire, don't read that here—but excitement in its deepest, most ineffable form.

THE STORY BETWEEN US

EVERY TIME MY children go out our front door they stand at the top of the porch stairs as if they've forgotten why they're there. When I ask why they don't just keep going, they say they're not aware of it; then make up reasons. "It's so we don't have to stand in the rain while you and Daddy go back and fuss about things. It's so we don't get wet while you lock the door." I smile at their goofy practicality, but still think it's something else. I think they've inherited my love of the in-between.

"Humans are threshold creatures of deep ambivalence," says John O'Donohue in *Beauty: The Invisible Embrace*. I like this—both the threshold (the option to go in or out) and the ambivalence (the space between decisions when all options are still open to you).

I got married October 13, 1991. A definite act, a crossing of a threshold, an apparent flush of certainty. Yes. Out of the billions of people on this earth, I want this one. The ceremony was in a friend's back yard. The marriage commissioner read a poem he'd written himself, so there was no "in sickness and in health," no "till death do us part"; and though he forgot his lines and, like a child in grade school, started over again, the only phrase either of us remembers clearly is "hills and valleys." We still look at each other once in a while, raise an eyebrow, say "hill or valley?" and move on. This is funny and everything's fine, but as it turns out, marriage is like a lot of other things in adult life: work, child rearing, paying bills. I alternate between feeling stunned by the banality and enormity of it, and wondering what it is I've gotten myself into.

"What is marriage about?" I asked a friend who'd been married for over thirty years. He paused, but only for a moment. "It's a story you make between you," he answered confidently. When I repeated the exchange to my husband, he looked momentarily peevish. "I don't have anything quite so poetic," he said. We were making dinner and then the kids came in, so I couldn't ask if he was threatened by poetry or if it was because it was a male friend I was quoting.

"You must not be friends with the opposite gender. You must reserve yourself for your mate," I read in a book about marriage, and scoff, thinking how much my male friends add to my life and perspective. But as I read on, doubt seeps in, and I think of the times I've harboured a what-if in my heart. What if those what-ifs are symptoms of some problem I'm avoiding? For my fiftieth birthday, friends brought poems they'd found or made, and one of my newer friends read a poem he'd written about me being somewhat wild and my husband bringing me in, and I wondered how did he know that? I thought it made me sound a little like a feral cat.

A while ago a female friend phoned me. She sighed and sighed again, and when I said, "What's wrong?" she said, "You know," and then because I didn't immediately, she explained, "The husband."

"Oh, that." I told her about another conversation with another wife during which we envied our single neighbours.

"Sometimes," my friend said, "I'd like it if he would just go away and maybe come back and visit once a year."

"It will pass," I said. Then because someone once told me my husband looked like Sting and that had made me think for the moment that I was part of something dramatic and eventful, I added, "He's very handsome." My friend was unmoved. "That doesn't help. I hate him."

All my married friends talk like this—all the women, that is. The men are strangely silent. What's with that? Is it some vestige of chivalry, or is it, as one man told me, that I'm just not one of them? When I asked my husband if he had trouble with being married sometimes, his eyes went all moony. When I told him to stop, he said he'd have to think about it. A little later he admitted, "Sometimes," then got romantic again quickly when I said, "Really?" perhaps with too much inflection. When I told him the more he admitted to ambivalence, the closer I felt to him, he laughed and changed the subject. I was a little annoyed that he'd skated away from me again, but not threatened. It was dinnertime, we were busy, and besides, I like when he turns a question around so I'm laughing, not at his answer, but at the way he's avoided the topic.

This makes it sound as if I don't want romance. I do. I want Heathcliff striding across the moors—all dark and broody and difficult. I want Heathcliff, not my husband, because Heathcliff would die for the love of me, and if I saw him striding across the moors or the soccer field for that matter, I'd know he was thinking about me and not the kids' soccer skills.

Some time ago, I read in the paper about a study that showed that married men live longer than single men, but that married women die sooner than their single counterparts. The results made perfect sense to me. My single friends and siblings—free to do whatever they want, go where they want— have lives that appear simple and attractive. Without the stress of continual negotiation and compromise, who wouldn't live longer? Forgive me, single people. These are the self-centred concerns of the permanently frazzled mind. Here, I'm certainly confusing the jagged nerve ends of my parenting self with my married self, but we had our children so early in our marriage, it's hard to disentangle that web. It's probably significant that I can't find this study. Instead, I find all sorts that tell me the opposite: that married women live longer than their single cohorts, and then, today, to add insult to this injury, I saw a headline announcing that caregivers live the longest of all. I must be an extremely vicious soul, because my first thought was that I'd rather die early and alone than spend my waning days changing my husband's diaper and spoon-feeding him. (Yes, I love him, but really? Is there no end?) I don't believe the people who write these articles have ever been caregivers, and a suspicious number of these findings are offered or published by religious organizations, so I'm curious again. Is it some sort of conservative conspiracy meant to keep us (generally longer-living, healthier) women in the kitchen?

For reassurance, I go to my bookshelf, where I find *The Power of Myth*, the Bill Moyers PBS interviews with Joseph Campbell. In my mind Campbell is a sort of über-man—fatherly, intelligent, kind. He calls marriage "the ordeal" and explains that by "ordeal" he means the sacrifice of self to something larger, to the relationship, not to the other. This sounds fair, rational, Solomon-like, something you both contribute to, like disaster relief or a reno project.

As I curl up on the couch with Campbell's invigorating mind, I add the idea of "ordeal" to "story" and consider whether in my understanding of them they clash or mesh. When I was little, my grandmother let us pile up on her white chesterfield for story time. She was a stern woman most of the time, but there on the chesterfield it was all about luxury. We'd cuddle in amongst the slippery cushions, and her voice with its rounded, Ottawa valley vowels would surround us. When the story ended, "and they lived happily ever after," I felt in my young mind a satisfying sense of completion and order: life was a journey; it could be a struggle (an ordeal), but eventually our separateness would end, and everything ever after would be the equivalent of slippery cushions, warm voices, and certainty.

Almost every summer our family piles into the contained space of the car and ventures into the uncontained spaces on the map. At the beginning, I enter this womb-like time with joy. By the end, I'm ready to get me to a nunnery.

I love my family. I also love being alone, and sometimes on holidays I'm visited by such piercing flashes of a solitary life that when I turn back to my family it feels like a decision I make, a conscious step across a line from self to other.

"Mother/wife/self, why does there have to be a line?" I imagine someone enlightened saying, someone like the Dalai Lama, or maybe Joseph

Campbell again, all white-haired and profound. "You are the line," my husband would add. "Walk it." There'd be that wink in his eye, the one that makes me laugh, forgiving almost everything.

On a recent holiday we camped at Bowron Lake, 3,000 feet above sea level in the BC interior. Our tent was pitched on the side of the lake with low hills rising all around us. It was midsummer and the blackflies had been making meals of us since we'd arrived, but every night when the sun dropped behind the horizon and the temperature with it, the flies disappeared, the sky got sharp and clear, and the stars emerged, like embers in black velvet. I sat by the fire with my husband and children, a warm tea bag pressed to my neck where the worst bites were.

We were into week three of our summer trip. We'd been to Haida Gwaii, where my husband and I had stripped down and walked into the sea, horrifying our children, who until then hadn't really understood what it meant to have parents who'd grown up in the seventies. We had stayed in the oldest cabin on North Beach, called the Ginger House. The kids were delighted by the rope between the loft and the main floor; I was delighted by the mismatched windows, the haphazard collection of pots on the haphazard shelves. Every day I had woken early to sit on the sand and watch the waves roll in, to marvel at the neat rolling folds in water, the birds skimming and rocketing along above them.

When we first arrived at Bowron, we drove to the public campground, but there was a "Bear in Area" sign, and the sites were mostly empty. I imagined the bear waiting in the shadows until our backs were turned, our children exposed and edible, hors d'oeuvres on a tray. We drove back to a private campground that was an open expanse of grass at the side of the lake, crowded with campers and trailers and tents like ours. It looked like a carnival. It looked like a place a bear would be embarrassed to be.

My husband, who has always taken bears in stride, along with the chores of finding firewood, flashlights, toilet paper, bug spray, and sleeping bags, looks on our summer camping trips as a time to read philosophy. He sat on one of our cheap folding chairs and held a large book on his lap. He looked relaxed in a way he rarely does at home, where the pressures of domesticity impinge on him too.

Every time we go camping he tells us about sleeping out in the snow when he was young. "It was great, no adults. We just had tarps and sleeping bags. We'd lie there and stare at the sky." We always ask, weren't you cold, and where were the adults, and how long did you stay, and I always picture him there, his mind bright with innocence, and sometimes I am charmed. But I have also heard this story so many times it's become part of the camping experience, as familiar as the smell of Coleman gas and the irritating ping of a tent peg hitting rock. When he suggested we do that on the beach by Bowron Lake, I reluctantly agreed. I was getting tired of the relentless pursuit of fun and thinking fondly of home and work. Still, I helped to lay the tarp and our sleeping bags out on the sand. The kids slid inside gleefully. My husband and I talked by the fire awhile, but I wanted some time alone in my head, so I went to the tarp and got in next to our sleeping kids.

It was so cold we'd worn hats and all our clothes to bed most nights. I'd slept lightly, muscles tense. Sandwiched between layers of tarp, my body heat reflecting back at me, I was warm for the first time on that trip, but that welcome feeling didn't prevent a small but persistent current of resentment from buzzing through the back of my brain.

My marriage is a good one, my husband a full partner in all the duties of domestic life—he cooks, he shops, he coaches soccer; I clean and also cook and shop, and I've made my work fit around the kids' schedules, so that I can be here for their lives. Sometimes I feel I've gotten the better part of this bargain; sometimes I wonder if I've become subsumed by everyone else's needs. As I lay unhappily in the dark, it seemed that after three weeks of togetherness my self was no longer clear on itself, the boundaries had become uncertain, the centre would not hold. I remembered earlier relationships, men I'd fallen in love with who had seen me as clay, something to mould. My husband had always seemed so amenable, so accommodating. Had all this fooled me into letting down my guard? Had some key element of my self leaked out so slowly I hadn't noticed it?

In *When Memory Speaks*, Jill Ker Conway says the myth of romantic love doesn't acknowledge a woman's need for work, for other satisfactions, like the ones men have—their hero stories. Women's stories (the traditional, the conventional, the persistent core of our culture) are about passivity; men's are about action. In men's stories, the love interest is the B plot. In women's stories, it's the A plot—as if solving the "which man?" question solves the question of "which life?" But there are other possibilities. Some women don't marry at all, and some choose a spiritual path. Nuns, says Conway, produced the first writing by women. They wrote of contemplation and of their attempts to become one with God or with spirit. I must have been in a cynical mood when I first read this, because I thought that it sounded as if the nuns were, like the conventional idea of wife, doing all of the work in the relationship. Was their writing an active engagement or was it a calculation: How do I make God love me? How do I make myself lovable enough for God? I know I'm skewing (or skewering?) one of the great human endeavours. I admire truly spiritual people, so why do I feel the need to fight against the idea of a higher authority all the time?

My husband came to the tarp bed, kissed me, and fell asleep. I lay and stared at the stars. A line from Joyce's *Ulysses* that a teacher had offered up earlier in the summer came to me: "The heaven tree of stars hung with humid night-blue fruit." It made sense, even the humid fruit, in a way I hadn't understood before.

Joseph Campbell says males and females follow separate paths towards the same goal: to transcend themselves. Like Odysseus, the man must go out from the home in search of his character. His is the hero's journey. Through battling demons, external and internal, he becomes both free of and larger than himself. Women, says Campbell, don't have to go out to find life. Life finds them. Menstruation, pregnancy, and childbirth are the demons that force women to become larger than themselves. So, here we are again. Our bodies, ourselves. Even Germaine Greer eventually wrote *Sex and Destiny*.

A rustling sound in the bushes behind us got louder. I heard the sand shifting near my head and reached for the flashlight, turned it on a pair of eyes and nearly jumped out of the bed, but my brain—which had leapt to *snake*—settled. It was a frog, dun green. "Look!" I said to my husband, meaning, "How can we sleep here? All manner of things could crawl in around our necks in the night." He grumbled, "It's only a frog," then went back to sleep, as I lay there trying to decide which would be worse, pulling some dry-skinned creature off my own body or my children's? My husband could take care of himself.

Campbell says not all men have to go out and slay dragons to be heroes. The man slogging from day to day to earn money to raise his family is also a hero. "But what about the mothers?" Moyers asks. "Yes, the mothers too," Campbell says, "but their stories are too common. Their stories are not news."

Not news?

Again the nuns flit through my vision, only this time I see their fierce strength. Maybe they're not simply praying to be adequate chalices for God's grace, but are the ultimate rebels, denying sex and destiny.

As I lay in the tarp thinking about the family I'd made on purpose, setting that against my pro forma resistance to order and convention, I wondered if all the stability in my life was good for me. Was I making the best of something, being passive? Or was I in the midst of a story I just didn't recognize?

"It's true," my husband said before he was my husband. We were in his apartment, the capacious ground floor of an old house. "It's true." He was kneeling above me on the bed, and the light behind him made his body look like a cross. I don't remember what we'd said before—it must have been something about love, and I must have been feeling open and vulnerable, and a little strange, because what I thought in that moment was that he was an angel and that I was finally safe, and then I wept.

Campbell calls this early recognition of love as "the seizure that comes in recognizing your soul's counterpart in another person." That sounds so nice. But of course after the first bloom of lust and romance fades you may wonder if it was a real seizure. The person you fell in love with is complicated, and when it comes down to it, you despair over the very qualities you first admired. What were you thinking? And now, what are you doing here?

According to the Vancouver therapist Toni Pieroni, that shuddering of the soul is recognition. People find partners with whom they can heal the fractured remains of childhood, she said. "Love is an intersection of dysfunctions," I replied, quoting an old friend. Pieroni laughed. "Exactly," she said, then explained that we get stuck at varying levels of emotional maturity depending on the environment we grew up in (the love environment, that is), and our subconscious self recognizes the familiar emotional territory in the partner. Pieroni referred me to a book called *Getting the Love You Want* by a Dr. Harville Hendrix. I didn't read it— Pieroni's intelligent précis of his theories was already weaving through my consciousness, and I was making up my own stories. I went back to Campbell, who says, "Duality is just the way we see things . . . everything in the field of time and space is dual." I find this comforting. In and out, love and hate, male and female—everything in pairs, everything with its opposite. Each moment we stand on a threshold and have to choose. "Every day you love and every day you forgive," Bill Moyers says, quoting the Puritans. "It is an ongoing sacrament—love and forgiveness."

On the beach in the tarp, I wasn't thinking about forgiveness or love. I was thinking about dysfunction and the scuttling sounds in the bushes behind us. The frog is a symbol of the unconscious—or, if you want to be a little rude, the male genitals. In Grimm's "The Frog Prince," the princess makes a deal with a frog and is rewarded when she finally loses her cool and throws him against a wall.

My husband slept, his unconscious apparently undisturbed. Meanwhile the stars burned (humid blue), a low cloud of fog settled on the lake, and it seemed in all this beauty that I was alone, and that this was wrong.

I have listened to too many romantic songs, seen too many movies, read too many books, or else I teeter somewhere, incomplete, on the ladder of emotional maturity, because at that point I imagined being with some other man, all that my husband is and more, someone who would think those thoughts with me—or would move me to new thoughts, not lie there beside me sleeping. I wondered if there were such men, and decided that other women were married to them already, and when I heard laughter from another campsite, I thought: there's one, then tried to remember the last time I had laughed so easily and freely. I reminded myself that my husband was the only man in this world who saw our daughter's brilliance and our son's depths, but it wasn't enough. I woke him. He snuffled a little, admired the stars, and all that was fine, but when he said something about the universe—even though I'd been thinking similar thoughts just half an hour earlier—it was all wrong. Probably no matter what he said it would have been wrong, but in that moment, it was so wrong and my discontent was so deep I slid out of the baggie bed and headed for the tent. Maybe after three weeks of twenty-four-hour togetherness all I needed was a little time to breathe my own air, which was surely true, but when I got there, and I was alone and cold, I decided what I really wanted was for him to come after me like Heathcliff would. "Jane!" he would cry, because his heart was breaking, his soul was trembling and he would surely die without me.

That didn't happen. I stood in the middle of our family-sized tent—the "two-room" model, which means there's a flap of fabric that's supposed to hang in the middle (as if that would make any difference). I was confused. I was tired. It was damn cold. The tent was mostly bare because the kids had taken their things to the tarp bed, but there were bits of clothing lying about. It was good to be alone—some part of me recognized this—a need as deep and elemental as hunger, but lack of sleep, lack of work, a surfeit of togetherness had put me so off kilter, I clung to romance as if to a lifebuoy. I remembered a long ago time when a lover did come after me. "But I love you!" he had cried with such conviction and surprise in his voice that we looked at one another as if the skies would open right then and there and change the things that didn't work between us.

John Stuart Mill wrote, "Most persons have but a very moderate capacity for happiness . . . and most persons are constantly wreaking that discontent which has its source internally, upon outward things."

"I can deal with you," my husband said to me some months before we married. We were in a ferry lineup. It was hot. The ferry was delayed. We were both uncomfortable and tired. He was smiling. "I can deal with you, too," I answered, smiling back and looking into his gentle eyes. My husband and I met in our thirties. We'd both weathered failures, miscalculations. On our first date we talked about our thoughts on marriage. It was an "I don't have much time, so I need to hear what you really think now" sort of conversation. Even before that date, I told him I didn't cook and that I liked country music sometimes. He's a jazz fan—I could almost hear him cringe, but didn't care. By then I'd learned if you don't give people a clear idea of yourself early on, they'll paint in the gaps to suit themselves.

I paced as much as I could in the tent, lay down, got up, folded the children's clothes. Still my husband didn't appear. At some level I knew he wouldn't. "Besides," he said, when I crawled in beside him and asked why he hadn't followed me, "I don't play games. I told you that at the beginning."

"It's not a game," I said, and meant it. I lay there waiting for him to comfort me, feeling cold and hard, certain that unless I got proof— absolute, sky-shattering proof that he loved me—the whole web-thin construct of our marriage was over.

While I was waiting, he fell asleep.

The sky grew slowly lighter, the line of hills beyond the lake, slowly sharper. Love isn't so much a choice as a force, I decided. First it busts us open, we are tender, vibrant, unbearably exposed. Some of us can tolerate being flayed open and live with that shimmery vulnerability, but others have to close up again quickly or at least put a scrim over it, a protective screen. Is romance part of that—a script to read from while burning? And what of other protective behaviours? Is that why I harbour the occasional what-if? Is it a way to shield me from the terrible openness at the core of love? A backup plan? "Nothing like the truth," a friend says to me over beer. We're talking about mothers and love, sitting by her propane heater, feeling the heat flare out from the blue, hissing flame, and shading our eyes from the glare of a neighbour's porch light. We laugh. Here is the love between friends who understand a mutual need for distance—love that lets you be, that doesn't press you too hard up against yourself.

In the morning my husband handed me a cup of coffee, in his smile all the equanimity of a well-built boat riding a wave. I smiled back. Why? This has happened before. I've been on the point of throwing things and storming out; then I've looked at him, and my anger has fallen away. "I can't stay mad at you," he said to me early on. I can't stay mad at him either, as it turns out. The friend who described marriage as an intersection of dysfunctions also used to say "I don't know how he puts up with you."

But aside from that, all my failings and flaws, are these moments all that sustain us? They seem too small, mere specks in time, iridescent, yes, miraculous, yes—but web thin, erratic, gossamer threads.

Campbell says we're all aiming for transcendence—transcending ourselves, transcending duality. He says we should not just love our enemies, but (metaphorically) swallow them so that we have their energy inside us. Does that mean I should swallow myself or my husband? Which of us is my enemy? The famous Groucho Marx line crosses my mind: "I wouldn't want to be part of a club that would have me as a member." My husband loves me. What's wrong with him?

After coffee my husband took the kids to a nearby stream to fish, and I went for a swim. The icy water hit my chest like a slap; for the first few strokes it felt like my lungs would stop, paralyzed by the cold. I did the breaststroke, keeping my head high out of the water as my mother used to. In this way we protect our hair. I recognize this common vanity too late, long after my mother's death. My son swims the same way, and I wonder is this concern for hair genetic, or are we part frog, with our legs moving so naturally into the frog kick? The frog has cold blood and a three-chambered heart; it's amphibious, thin skinned, sensitive. Maybe I see it as a family emblem because I relate to it.

In the campsite next to us, a man stood knee deep in the water with his son. They were playing with boats. His wife was busy at the camper with food and their baby. She called out, "Breakfast!" and he called back, "Okay!" He turned to his boy and splashed, and the boy giggled, and they walked back into the shore. They were in the midst of it all, the smaller children boot camp. I imagined by their calm voices that they'd accepted this—the diapers, the little plastic boats, the endless cry and trill of small voices around them. Who knew, they probably said to each other, when their babies were in bed at the end of another long day, who knew we'd end up here?

Maybe it's not that big a deal, and marriage is just a parcel, a package agreement. I'll take care of you; you'll take care of me. "Love is compassion," Joseph Campbell says, coming out of ourselves and feeling another's pain. I have, on occasion in our marriage, felt love shoot through me when I've seen my husband in pain—emotional or physical. Maybe need is what love is about. We love people because we can be useful to them.

I studied the rocks at the edge of the shore; they were themselves whether they were in or out of the water. I thought of a stone threshold in a relative's home, the appearance of softness where a hundred years' worth of feet passing over it have worn a shallow curve.

My parents separated after thirty-three years of marriage. I think my father missed my mother; I'm not sure she missed him. On TV one night

I watched the dying June Callwood in an interview. She talked of the stages of marriage: the working stage when the children were young as a challenge, but the ending, when both are old, as "sweet." "We are tender with one another," she said. "It's worth it."

The water, after a while, felt almost warm. I swam the length of the beach to the small river at one end of it. My children were on the shore with their father. They joined me in the small rapids. Their father, not such an amphibious creature, stayed on the land.

I studied him as he stood on the shore watching us, the family we'd made on purpose. He looked handsome in the morning light. He was smiling, making some small joke with the kids. I thought of the way we came to edges and then laughed again. I thought of Heathcliff and how attractive he appears leaning into the wind, battling some dark, unknowable demon of his own. My husband doesn't need saving. He is not Heathcliff. He is not a frog, and he is not a prince. He is himself. Life, day to day, is full of recognitions and then thresholds—vantage points of the in-between, places to consider the changing light and gather courage before turning the next page (that great act of will and hope) in the story between us.

SHAPE

W E SWITCHED OUR kitchen table last week and went from round to rectangular. Now our family of twenty-one years faces one another across a smaller expanse. "It's changed things," our son says, looking at us in a way that reminds me of when he was six months old, his head turning from one to the other, his face open and observant. "Now," he says, "it makes it more intense. It makes it confrontational."

My husband and I are having a discussion about fathoms because our son has just used the word. He and his sister are sailors, so we hear this kind of language sometimes: knots, fathoms, breech. "What is a fathom?" my husband asks. "Maybe it's eight feet," I say, taking a guess, thinking there's something literary and complete about eight. My husband says, "No. It's not eight. It's something like three." In his tone, I think I hear dismissal. Our son gets up from the table and comes back with the iPad. "It's six feet," he says, after a moment. "See?" I say, turning to my husband. "I was way closer than you." He looks back with such apparent calm, something in me busts open, and a little dam of peevishness and frustration busts open. "How can you just announce something like that without knowing a bit more than I did? As if my idea is completely ridiculous. That's a perfect example of male bravado, which goes careening about the world full of nothing more than hot air that blusters and blunders and rams up and rolls over and squashes all sorts of things?"

My family watches, waiting for the rant to end, my son directly across the table from me, his face impassive, intelligent, unalarmed. These miracles, my children. How have they emerged from the turmoil of me so apparently unscathed? My family doesn't know that I've just been rejected for a piece of writing I had high hopes for. After a rejection, I feel as if my insides are showing through. I speak with the voice of the oppressed. I feel oppressed, though I'm not. I live the life of a privileged white woman in one of the wealthiest countries (and cities) in the world. Sure, one of the rooms smells of dead rodent (something died in the walls), and it's dusty and grimy in places because I, the oppressed, refuse to spend my days cleaning, and because I, the oppressed, also refuse to spend my days nagging at other people. It's tiresome to nag. I'd rather live with the dirt, which is healthy, to a degree. A little dust, a little grime. Not going to kill anyone. Besides, haven't I read over and over that if you're a woman and you want to be a writer, you need to let go of the housework?

Every other week or so, my husband, who will also claim oppression here—given a chance—gets out the mop and scrubs the kitchen floor. I ignore the kitchen floor, other than to sweep or vacuum it once in a while, figuring the dirt just sinks nicely into the wood, giving it more patina.

Our old kitchen table was round. Sitting around it, we were set at angles from one another, like pieces of a pie, our attention going towards the centre or across at one another. We had energetic conversations, and sometimes we laughed so hard our daughter would fall off her chair. We still laugh, but now my husband and I sit on one side of the table, the children on the other, and we watch them, as if at a show, as they talk to one another, and I'm not sure because this isn't a scientific observation, not calibrated and considered, but it seems to me that they talk more, and sometimes elbow one another and sometimes exchange a look of such shared knowledge and experience that I want to weep for the beauty of it. My husband and I also share looks with one another, and it's different, true. I have to turn my head to look at him, but then I feel the purpose in that, the decision I make, wanting to see his face, and that, too, feels remarkable, surprising, a confrontation of yes.

SEMANTICS

CAVE

L AST SUMMER MY family and I visited the Horne Lake caves on
Vancouver Island. I'm claustrophobic. The idea of going into a dark,
confined space filled me with horror. Before we headed up the trail, my
son and I had a moment by the car. I handed him a helmet. What do you
think? I said. "Well, I'm scared," he said, "but we're here, so we might as
well do this." The being there was because he'd been vibrating off the
walls in the picturesque little cabin we'd rented on the beach. After three
days of quiet walks by the sea and reading, he was ready to put antifreeze
in our dinner. We put on the hard hats, checked the small lights on top of
them. The entry to the cave was a vertical slit in the side of a forested
slope. There was no sign, no instructions. My husband and I, who had
expected some guiding in this self-guided tour, explored farther along the
path and found nothing. We watched our son squeeze in and followed. I
thought it would be a dead end, that we'd find the real cave somewhere
else, along some other path. I imagined some large opening in the hillside,
a sign with a map, friendly advice on spelunking, a few general warnings
about lights and telling other people where you were. A few feet past this
chest-compressing entry, the space opened to a small cavern, tall enough
for us to stand upright. The woman who'd rented us the helmets—a
fiercely outdoorsy sort of person with sinewy muscles and intelligent
eyes—had told us to look for the spiders that lived on the roof of the cave.
"There's hundreds of them," she said. "Look up."

The spiders were small with black bodies and legs. Attractive as far as spiders go. They were neat looking, almost circular in shape. I could have been happy to end our tour there, but our son found a passage farther in. "This way," he called, his voice excited. As I watched him and followed, fear making every cell in my body vibrate as if an electric current was running through, I didn't know if I was prouder of him for telling me he was afraid or for putting his fear aside so easily, like it was a package he could box up and ignore.

Caves don't have neat outward curving walls as they do in the movies. The walls hump in and get in the way. They're wet; moisture trickles down them. Everything's on a slant. You can't walk straight. You walk with your feet on a narrow, pebbly floor, a stream really, sole-deep. You're glad of boots. One hand has to support your right side, so you're crawling in a crab-like scramble. The brochure said this cave went in a hundred feet to a ladder and a waterfall. This sounded attractive, dramatic. The brochure had glossy pictures, smiling faces under hard hats. My daughter walked in front of me, small enough to stand up straight. I was thinking of the roof above us, the rock slanting. My heart was speeding up, beginning to beat fluttery and light. Up ahead, an enormous boulder blocked the tunnel, a small space on one side. My son had already disappeared around it.

"Just wait, Colin!" I called. My husband called out too. I was grateful for this. I wasn't crazy to worry that I couldn't see him. That we were under the earth somewhere, and there was only the woman with sinewy muscles who knew where we were.

My daughter stopped in front of me. "I don't like this," she said. "I don't want to be here." My husband paused. "It's okay, Liv. Just breathe. Take a step at a time. We're fine." We were not fine. My heart was pounding. I could feel my body pressing in, the blood and thoughts pounding. I imagined turning the other way and going out, but decided if my family was going to be crushed in the earth I would have to be crushed with them.

"We're okay," my husband said again to our daughter. His voice was light and calm. I loved and hated him for being so good at calming her down that she started walking again. I followed, telling myself that the rock wall inches from my face was stable. There were no rumbles, no tremors. I would not think of such things. I would think about breathing. It was not the first time I've thought that if I didn't have children, I could be enjoying a quiet life, reading about other people's adventures or thinking about my own, long past. On the other side of the tumour, my son said, "Come on around, Dad. It's cool over here." I knew why he was talking to his father. He'd already given up on me, and while there's a little pang of regret in this, I'm glad they have this thing to share, this ability to maintain curiosity and excitement against rising panic and potential disaster.

My husband squeezed around the tumour on the left. I watched our daughter, thinking surely she wouldn't follow. I was silent. I would not impose more of my fear; though surely it was vibrating off the walls by then. I ached for her to stop. I thought the two of us could go back to the entrance and wait for them. No shame in that, though I was aware of the gender stereotypes—males forging ahead, females retreating and worrying. How did I end up like this? Didn't I read *The Second Sex* at seventeen and start yelling at men shortly after? Have I stopped yelling at men? More important, have I stopped keeping up? Our daughter moved forward. Damn. Really. Damn. I hated doing this. The tumour was a soft beige colour. Was it sandstone? It was wet. What if it dissolved right then, my rain jacket the final, busting touch that set off the crushing flush of wet sand? We'd all die, me first, breathing sand.

The other side of it was bigger, my family waiting for me there. I smiled, pretending bravery. "Cool," I said. My vocabulary so abysmal. As if I'd been medicated and forced to read nothing but sixties magazines for the past forty years, overlaid with a steady diet of parenting manuals exhorting me to listen to my children, to be steady and consistent and brave. For the latter, I've ascended mountains, surfed, descended into a mine, now the cave. Several summers ago, I held a tarantula in my hand, in front of a crowd of toddlers. In spite of all that, my family knew I was lying. But I was there. I hoped that was enough.

My husband said, "This is great, isn't it? We should have brought the camera." Our son was already scrambling forward, where the walls slanted in again. I followed. Miserably. Fighting off death thoughts. Fear thoughts. Battery-dying thoughts, thoughts of the dark closing in behind us, the tunnel lengthening out.

After the male half of my family had satisfied themselves that we'd reached the end of the cave, we turned back. At first it was familiar enough: the tumour, the narrow, slanting crab-walk space. The cave had twisted left after leaving the first cavern, so we knew we had to turn right to get back, but there were dark folds in the rock. Some of these looked like paths. Our lights seemed to assault the rock, gleaming wetly, smashing light particles back at us in narrow funnelled beams, while at the edges everything fell away again into its natural darkness. My family wasn't far from me, but I couldn't see them. I went into one of the creases and came to a dead end. Panic flared in my chest, as if a bird were caught there flapping its wings.

I found them in the vestibule of the cave considering spiders. "There's some kind of bug that eats its own legs when it can't find food, and then the legs grow back," my husband said. "That's gross," our daughter replied, and then we talked about how that would work. Would the energy gained by eating the leg be greater than the energy used in creating a new one? Was this just a temporary measure? "I'll just eat my leg for now until something better walks by," I said.

"I want to go back in," our son said and disappeared into the dark again. My husband followed.

My daughter and I looked at one another and walked outside. We stood in the open, the trees spiking up, the wide open empty sky above us. Everything normal again. We smiled at one another. It felt good, but deflating, and I thought about how terror had heightened everything, forcing me to see each moment in tiny focused shards. Outside in the open air, the moments were spread out around me, blurred and amorphous and empty except for what I could make of them.

GHOSTS

I DIDN'T WANT TO write this essay. Breakdown. Middle age. How depressing is that? But I like writing. Putting words around an event is like putting wrapping paper and ribbon around a gift—do a good job and it makes even the most questionable choice look celebratory and certain. My injury was not life-threatening. A mere fillip, a twist of a knee, a bite of bone into soft tissue—nothing ultimately damning, nothing more insidious than a degrading of the infrastructure. In the years since it happened, I've paid attention and I've tried not to, but soft tissue damage is like a cabal of old ghosts who won't leave, boring as hell, but a message the mind can't ignore. I've iced, elevated and exercised, consulted friends, sports doctors, and physiotherapists, and had surgery. It still hurts, and I'm still unwilling to admit it as more than a temporary phenomenon. What I hope is that this essay will help me make peace with it—help me take the new measure of body and mind, or at least locate the "now you're middle-aged" set of operating instructions.

Marni Jackson in her book *Pain: The Fifth Vital Sign* says that pain fuses the body and mind, and that it is something like a river, pulling tributaries of older pains into the flow of fresh insult, so that a person stung by a bee, for instance (as she was—inspiring her to write the book), will remember and feel other pains, including emotional ones. How right she is. With this injury, relatively minor though it is, I am pulled into an old image of myself, something I thought I'd long outgrown—a person who injures herself, accident prone? Apt to hurl herself into situations she can't control? And then happy to go home and be cared for by her mother?

When I injured my knee at fifty, there was no hope of my mother taking care of me again, but perhaps the ghosts (maybe even her ghost) had other things in mind. It's common, says Jackson, for women to injure themselves on the cusp of menopause; it's part of the general chaos caused by surging and ebbing hormones. I like this idea—partly because it takes some of the responsibility away from me (screwing up again) and partly because it makes me think that women aren't so different from men. Men buy sports cars when they're confused about aging. Women go out and jump out of airplanes or take up motorcycling. Either way it's the same: we're all leaping at old ideas of ourselves.

When my friend Janet and I decided to take a backcountry ski trip with the kids, there was a definite whiff of "let's prove we're not dead yet" about our plans. We were both fifty at the time, both, as it happened, menopausal. Over the years we'd known one another, we'd talked of the adventures we'd had in our youth. So in a bloom of fresh bravado and confidence we set off with our kids to a place Janet had gone twenty years earlier. The first couple of hours on the trail were fine—snowflakes feathering out of the sky, kids excited and chattering, skis sliding easily forward and up. As the afternoon wore on and the temperature rose, snow began sticking to the base of skis, mostly mine and my ten-year-old daughter's, so that soon every other step required a smack with a ski pole to release the stubborn clumps gathered underfoot, making it like trying to walk on high heels in snow. After a couple of hours we were only about halfway there. As we stood by the side of the lake and tried to see where the trail began again on the other side, I thought of other trips in mountains and felt the same sense of fear and awe.

There's no point pretending that going out into the wild is anything less than a test. The clever gadgets and bright clothing in the outdoor equipment stores make us feel as though we're in control, but when we get out there, when there's nothing but mountains and trees, when the trail markers are gone, the sky is a uniform grey and the wind is suddenly pressing into your face like a hand, you are alone with whatever mix of knowledge, experience, strength, and courage, or lack of it, that you bring. "I bet the trail's right across there," Janet said, pointing towards the opposite shore, which to me looked like trees and more trees. "It's March. I'm sure the ice is fine," she added. I knew I was revealing myself for the coward I am, but couldn't stop imagining one of us sinking helplessly into the lake, pinned by skis and pack. As we slogged back along the shore towards the trail we'd left, feeling depressed and tired, a man dressed head to toe in bright blue shot out of the woods and onto the lake like some sort of angel of backwoods mercy. He looked as if he'd been trusting the frozen surface of that lake all his life. We followed him and asked if he knew the way to the cabin. He said he'd lead us there.

The trail on the other side (exactly where Janet had predicted it would be) was longer than we thought: it wound endlessly through the woods with several dips and turns and rising hills. Our long skis got caught on sharp corners. When we fell, our packs pinned us down like upside-down beetles. At one point my daughter and I fell at the same time. If she hadn't been crying already, I would have. My muscles, worn from the gut-draining flu I'd had just before the trip, were played out. I lay in the snow wondering if I could ever move again. I thought of people who go to sleep in the snow. It seemed like a good idea. But I got up, chivvied my daughter to get up, and then my son appeared, bright faced and full of energy, and told us he'd seen the cabin just up ahead. As we clumped up to it, the man in blue emerged. He'd waited to make sure we arrived safely, then shot off again before we could thank him.

Inside the cabin we put a Therm-a-Rest on a bench so Olivia could lie down. I longed to lie down too, but there was only the floor and a table—besides, there was work to be done. To get to the firewood stored under the cabin, we had to prop up a heavy slab of floor. "We could put the ladder down there," Janet said, studying the ground about seven feet below. "Nah, it's okay. I've got it," I said impulsively, and dropped down to the dirt. I was trying to make up for being such a wimp at the lake and for wanting nothing more than to lie down somewhere, preferably next to the fire, and groan. I missed my husband, who might have indulged such behaviour, and I missed heat. I found the wood and handed it up to Janet easily enough, but then there was the problem of getting back up. At first I thought it was hopeless and imagined being trapped down there all night, but then found some purchase on a piece of lumber extending from a dark corner of the underfloor and used that to manoeuvre my way up.

After, I felt inordinately proud and excited by this small physical feat. See? I told myself. You're still young. This sudden springing idea of youth helped me move through the next hours. We kept a fire going, and the kids sat on the benches close to it. Janet and I went out to the lake to get water. The wind had died and the lake was a sheet of white. Beyond it the sun was sinking towards the hills, and the light was turning soft and golden. I didn't take a picture of Janet, but I should have. She looked emblematic, a lone figure in white space. I felt proud of us. We'd made it. That night we ate well, but when we all finally lay down in the loft, and I waited for my body to let go of its irritated buzz of exhaustion, the expected feeling of calm didn't arrive; instead my mind whirled with worries. What on earth had we been thinking, bringing five kids into the wilderness? What if the snow was just as sticky tomorrow? What if there was a storm? What if one of them got hurt? What if . . . what if . . . the thoughts circled all night.

In the morning, Janet said she hadn't slept either. "What were you worrying about?" I asked. "Bats in the rafters," she said. We looked at one another and laughed.

Over three hundred years ago, René Descartes came up with the theory that our minds and bodies are separate entities. He decided this while meditating in a bread oven, apparently, possibly not taking into account that his body needed the warmth of the oven for his mind to be able to concentrate. But never mind. Aside from contemplating that Cartesian philosophy came from a man in an oven, Descartes' theory that our minds and bodies are separate seemed for many generations to be perfectly reasonable. In *Pain*, Jackson describes this long-held belief as the "forklift" approach: our brains the managers, our bodies the workers. Most of us still think this way, but scientists now recognize that there's a lot more brain in our bodies than we've previously acknowledged. A person who loses a limb still feels the limb in the brain. A blind person learns to "see" through sensors placed on the tongue or the back of the knee. This is termed "plasticity," and the brain is considered a shifting, adaptable organ. Thoughts and stimuli (chemical, biological, ephemeral) move in and through it. Every thought leaves a trail, every movement begins with a thought. So as Janet and I lay there with our bodies so tired and our minds so awake, was it an unrooted, immaterial emotion keeping us awake, or lactic acid?

This isn't as far-fetched as it sounds. Although we've long thought that lactic acid hinders us (think of how stiff your muscles are after exercise), it's actually what keeps us moving. Without it, potassium—a waste product of aerobic exercise—would block the nerve pathways to the brain, and our muscles would literally be paralyzed. Excess lactic acid goes to the brain, where it's used as fuel to keep our minds sharp while we're running from those sabre-toothed tigers. Maybe Janet and I couldn't sleep because we still had lactic acid in our brains, which is a little like trying to sleep in a place where a kid has pulled the fire alarm.

The next morning, glad to be up and doing instead of lying down and thinking, I took a candle and rubbed it on the bases of our skis. "What are you doing, Mum?" my daughter asked. "Fixing our skis." I handed her a candle. We pretended we were drawing pictures on the bases. The wax felt warm in my hand, reminding me of family ski weekends when I was young, happy debates about snow temperature and wax colour. The candle happened to be red, just right for the conditions, I told my daughter—not mentioning that with candles, the colour was meaningless; no matter, it worked. When we set off, the mood among the kids was light and hopeful. The return to the lake was mostly downhill, the boys whooped and hurtled down the short, steep sections of the curving trail we'd struggled up so unwittingly the day before. They laughed if they fell in the deep powder to the side. My daughter manoeuvred each challenge less joyfully, but was competent and certain. Janet and I moved cautiously. We both knew we couldn't afford to injure ourselves this far away from the road and help. "Right," Janet said, "we can't let them get too far ahead of us." She managed the first part of the hill but fell to the side at the bottom. I was so focused on getting to her that I didn't fall. The next slope was steeper. Janet made it down; then it was my turn.

Einstein proved that conventional notions of time are meaningless. I don't understand his theories in a scientific sense, but often feel the emotional truth of them. Thirty years earlier, when I had the downhill accident, I'd rocketed from the lip of a long curling hiccup in the hill and rose in a pure line like a vector in a math problem: 120-pound female, 60 mph, 20-foot drop. How long was I in the air? How far did I fly? For how long? Maybe it doesn't matter. I experienced flight, which makes me feel lucky and amazed. How many people get to fly? Lots, I suppose, if you poll extreme athletes, but one of the things I've learned from that experience is that I'm neither extreme nor, truly, an athlete. I was lucky to fly, but lucky also to come out of it relatively intact. Einstein would have been able to explain what happened to me in the air, the way time seemed to expand so that I could think and register three things: surprise at breaking free of gravity, concern over a man scurrying out of the way some twenty feet below me, and crushing fear that I would spend the rest of my life in a wheelchair. I think I blacked out before hitting the ground—sheer terror shutting my mind closed. I came to sliding down the hill on my side, still at speed, not feeling any pain yet, but whimpering, afraid my rag of a body would hit a tree next or another bump.

Neurologists say injury reshapes the brain. Existentialists say experiences make us who we are. More than thirty years later, my flight and crash are still hard for me to contemplate; is that because my brain has changed or because I just don't like to remember pain?

Janet descended the next steep slope successfully. I teetered at the top of it, considering. I had gone back to downhill skiing the season after my accident and told myself this meant I'd fully recovered, but my skis had never been out of my control for more than a split second since, and I had never had more than a minor fall. This was a tiny slope; in theory, I had the experience and the strength to manage, but my mind wasn't so certain. I was fifty, out of shape, a mother, a part-time teacher. My idea of myself was no longer shaped by how many sit-ups I could do and how fast I could run gates. We were still miles from the car, potentially vulnerable, but the slope was about the same pitch as the slope in a starting gate. So I placed my poles down the slope in front of me and imagined a timing bar at my shins. Then I counted a quiet "5, 4, 3, 2, 1" and propelled my body forward, leaving my shins to cross the timer last. It worked. I became a teenager on a race-course again, feeling excitement instead of fear, the pull of gravity and the building speed an opening into something new, rather than a freefall into disaster.

As I write, this seems like not that big a deal; it wasn't, I suppose, just another of the ordinary tricks that our minds play, accessing memory or some earlier version of self—but at the time it seemed to me miraculous and startling, the flashbacks as real to me as this moment, sitting in the car in the cold Vancouver fog waiting for my son's soccer game to begin.

These flashbacks were so intense and I liked them so much that I was almost disappointed when we reached the lake. From there it was easy, the trail widened. Soon we were only about a mile from the car. The boys goofed around in the deep snow. My daughter skied on, head down, making one stern and steady turn after another. I recognized determination in her stiff posture, not pleasure. She wanted to get home, get out of there. There is something both magnificent and terrifying in having a child who reminds you so much of yourself. In her I see courage but also recognize a capacity for error, and can sometimes see her mistakes just before they're about to happen. She fell, her skis twisted under her, and she started to cry. I thought I was keeping my mind focused on getting to her, but I must have had a flash of mother-to-the-rescue in my brain, or worse.

Our lives are circles, we go around whether we like it or not. When we meet ourselves on the backside of the circle, perhaps there's awareness, at some point even forgiveness, maybe even learning. We hope for learning. I thought I had learned not to hurt myself anymore, to slow down, to focus when I was in situations where injury could occur. I thought I'd also learned to see myself not as the athlete my mother wanted me to be, but as something less clear than that, someone less easy to categorize: ordinary, in other words, with the usual shares of grace and clumsiness, ability and flaw.

In the downhill race, just before a key part of the course where I was meant to jump over the lip in the hill, I hit some chatter marks. My skis rattled under me, and instead of thinking "Jump," I thought, "I'm going fast." That moment of distraction caused my accident. If I had jumped, I might have finished the race. Some said I might even have won it, but what else would they say on their mission of kindness, visiting me in hospital, seeing the magnitude of my mistake right in front of them? I looked like a toppled Statue of Liberty, without the dignity and the laurels, my left arm raised above my head, plaster extending from my wrist down to my hips.

I wonder now if my accidents are caused not just by distraction but also by hubris. I see this ghost bending down to smile at me (tall, dark, fatally attractive) as he sticks out a foot to trip me. As I hurried through the deep, heavy snow towards my daughter, I was thinking how lucky it was that I'd mastered gravity with skinny skis, overlarge boots, and a heavy pack. Then I fell over to the side and heard the pop inside my knee. As pain flashed like fire up to my hip, I knew I'd entered the complex and unsolvable world of soft tissue damage. I'd become a person like so many others, a person with a bad knee. Aristotle said pain is punishment—this seemed fitting as I lay there cursing myself—shouldn't I, of all people, know better than this? What sort of mother was I if I couldn't even get to my child?

Janet yelled, "Are you all right?" I answered an embarrassed no and packed snow against my knee, as my son hiked up the hill towards me, and my daughter stopped crying and untangled her twisted limbs. After a couple of minutes, the pain subsided from a screaming ten on the scale to about eight. I wriggled out of my pack and manoeuvred my body upright, carefully trying a little pressure on the leg—afraid it would set off another searing flash. It didn't. The pain had settled to burning coals. Janet pulled a tensor from her pack and wrapped my knee expertly, then found a length of rope so she could drag my pack behind her. So with me skiing like a flamingo and Janet towing my pack behind her like a corpse, we travelled the last mile to the parking lot without further drama. In the car Janet produced some powerful painkillers. By the time we reached the ferry, my leg felt like it was floating, and I was in a post-injury state of calm.

When you're young, you can't see patterns because you haven't lived them yet. In middle age, the future, depending on your mood and where you're looking, can seem like a sunny meadow or a bog full of pit vipers and quicksand. I have so much experience at being a patient I could put it on my CV: "works well with doctors," "tolerant of hospital food." I went home and put my leg up. I thought a few days of ice and rest would make it better. A year later, still limping, I had surgery. Operation number 13 for the CV. A knee is an intersection of bones and cartilage, a weight-bearing intersection, a hinge. Knees can be damaged with blows or hard twists, ligaments can tear; the cartilage can rip. In other parts of the body, blood would carry healing cells to the damaged area, but in knees, especially the inner core, there's no blood flow, so if there's a tear or crack or bruise, the healing is slow or nonexistent. An MRI showed a tear in my meniscus. My GP, who's known me for years, said, "Why haven't you had surgery yet?"

I have surgery. It's a day procedure. I'm in and out and then on crutches for a time, a familiar state of being. What's not familiar is that the surgeon gives me a videotape of the operation, so afterward my family and I sit on the couch and watch as the head of my femur appears on our TV, pale and glowing, like a full moon on a clear night. "The head of your femur looks very nice," a voice on the TV says, and I recognize the slight lilt of the surgeon's voice, his sure, precise way of speaking. He explains that he's inserted three instruments into my knee through narrow metal tubes: the camera, a probe, and a small grinder, which looks to my mind like a set of shark's teeth. On the TV the bone slides out of view and my muscle tissue appears, pink and bright, then the ligaments—thick white bands that glisten like the inside of an oyster shell. In the background, against a muscle wall, there's a small, darker red shape that looks like a flatfish. Along the edges, long, feathered bits of white matter move in the currents of water that were pumped into the joint so the surgeon could see better. "This is synovial matter," the surgeon says. "It's normal." I think it looks like veils fluttering in the wind, one of them like an anemone with its feelers trailing out. "Your meniscus looks fine," he says, "but you have a lot of synovial matter."

Some time later, cutting meat off a bone for soup, I recognize the joint and have to press my mind away from thinking of the red tissue under the knife as muscle like my own. I'm thinking vegetarianism, animal rights, the plastinated bodies I'd seen at the *Body Worlds* exhibit. The pig's bone looks beautiful too. I recognize ligament, feel its rubbery strength and study how it funnels into a furrow in the bone. I tug to see how firmly it's attached; then I pull the joint apart and find the plate of yellowish tissue, which must be the meniscus. I'm not able to investigate further—the flesh in front of me is too familiar, and I decide I've gone far enough. I quickly chop the meat into small pieces and consign the bone to the garbage, not letting myself think of the pig and its short and sturdy life.

Pain, of course, is more than Aristotle's idea of punishment; it's a glimpse of mortality. Each time my knee hurts I'm aware of limits, the pain a symbol of my failure to manage myself—an accident, sure, but something I could have prevented, if I'd been smarter?

Recently, at coffee with a friend, she said we need to let ourselves be open with our friends, they love us whether we're strong or not. Maybe we need to love ourselves too. My memories of injury are stamped in; so too, perhaps, are the ghosts, who after four years of knee pain have their own armchairs and footstools. They read books, they drink tea. The knee still hurts. I have problems with my back at times. The list could go on. It's not interesting. It's the same as most, much lesser than many. Maybe the pain needs a footstool too. When I visited the surgeon for a post-surgery checkup, he told me the cartilage under my kneecap had been bruised in my fall and that it was most likely the cause of my pain. There was nothing much he'd done in the operation to help that, he added; then told me it would heal of its own accord in about two years. "So, was it worth going in?" I asked, afraid I might offend him with this question—afraid, too, of his answer.

"Now we know how to treat it," he said. "Now we know exactly what is wrong."

I limped away, thinking, true, there was some comfort in this. The naming of pain, like the naming of ghosts—a sense of settling. My ghosts seem to agree. Not that there's peace in there. Not that there will ever be an end to the wrestling we all have to do—maybe with middle age it's just this: your thoughts have shades and shadows. You could call it depth. You could call it a pack of ghosts and decide they're there to keep you from getting cocky or stupid again. Either way, life makes ghosts. The trick may be in learning how to move forward anyway and sometimes, even, to dance with them.

A LEAP AND A BLESSING

I DON'T TAKE PUBLIC TRANSIT very often, which is a failing—not just environmentally, but also personally, because sometimes that forced contact with the rest of the populated world can be profound. In Japan, many years ago, I was trapped in the small space between train cars by a crowd of schoolboys; my claustrophobia reached such a level that one leg began to judder up and down like the needle on a sewing machine, and the only thing that prevented me from climbing out over the tops of my fellow passengers' heads was the gaze of a man about a foot away who conveyed calm to me by keeping his eyes trained on mine.

When something like this happens I'm struck by how effectively people communicate without language, and then I get to wondering what it is that allows us to do that. I don't get very far, but the question niggles, so when I see articles about the brain or genetics, I always stop and read them. Today, for instance, I read that our genes are not necessarily fixed, as we've so far believed: that we aren't just shells to transport genetic code from one generation to the next. What we have is more like a caretaker role. Not only do we need to keep ourselves alive long enough to reproduce, but we must also think good thoughts, eat well, behave in a sensible manner and in all ways be as good to our bits of genetic coding as, say, we should be to the land and water that support us.

Here we are. The Broadway SkyTrain station. East Vancouver, a little shabby, a little noisy and crowded, but a place that's alive, not tamed into stultifying sameness—good for my DNA? I get on the train and find a seat near the door. As I settle in, a large, gangly man rushes in and clumsily sits on the pull-down chair on the other side of the doorway. He must have bumped the people in the seat next to him because a pleasant but sardonic voice loudly proclaims, "It's okay. We're just Native people." Did I hear anger in his tone? As well as reading the article on DNA, I'd heard something on the radio about it being Aboriginal Day. At the time I'd barely noted it, but now I wonder if this encounter will be emblematic somehow. Will the Native man expound on what it is to be Native in Canada, and are the rest of us on the train going to be asked to bear witness to an act of reconciliation or retribution?

"I'm okay," the gangly man says in response. The non sequitur doesn't seem to concern the Native man, who continues to talk in a loud voice about nothing and everything—people who are always late for things, the weather, friends. We have long passed the time when the announcement should sound and the doors close. When a train official walks onto our car, I assume he's coming to speak to the loud talker, perhaps to point out the importance of voice modulation? The official is dressed in the white uniform they wear, a little like parking attendants, bellhops or White Spot employees. He's slight and curved, a middle-aged man with a rounding belly, his neat hair and moustache going grey, his eyes confident, almost smiling, a man who knows what his job is and how he's going to do it. As he walks towards the talkers, I wonder whether he has practised this look in front of the mirror, or does it come naturally to him? Has he been blessed by a solid sense of himself, has his DNA been well fed with self-esteem, good food and a loving mother?

"Did someone here go down onto the tracks just now?" the man says in a voice loud enough to fill the car. Even though the trajectory of his voice is clear, there's a long enough silence after he stops speaking that I am reminded of similar moments in school when the teacher (not nearly so calm or quietly polished) threatened detention for all of us unless someone fessed up *now*. It may be my imagination, but I think the entire car of adults is being rocketed back to grade 6 with me.

Just when I'm wondering what sort of threat a SkyTrain man could offer (I didn't see any weapons), the gangly man calls out in a calm voice, "I did. I dropped my phone." The official nods, he's calm, too, and pleasant; the quiet Canadian air of the train will not be interrupted, not by him. "Would you step outside for a minute, please," he says, and the man gets up clumsily. He's too big for himself, too long in the limb, his clothes flap and waver as though the engine that drives him can only start with jerks and stutters, but eventually he moves off the train with the official. They stop a few feet away on the platform, and the train doors remain open. I lean toward them, straining to hear. What will the gangly man say? What went through his mind before he jumped down onto the tracks? His apparent lack of fear might be ignorance, but what if he had studied the situation before making his leap? I wonder what it would be like to live inside a mind like that, if life would feel like a continual adventure, every moment bristling with potential. And then, if I were suddenly to give up a lifetime of modulation, would it affect my DNA?

The two men continue to talk, face to face, their voices indistinguishable in a low rumble—it seems the whole car is leaning towards them when the official's voice sounds clearly: "I just want to know who you are."

Just then, the train doors close with no warning bell and the train glides out of the station. The Native man says to the woman beside him, "I wouldn't want to tell him who I am," and then he says more things that I cannot hear over the gathering speed and noise of the train. I am thinking of prejudices (why had I immediately assumed it was the loud-talking Native man who was causing the delay?). As we round the curve past Science World, the Native man stands up. "Happy Aboriginal Day, everyone!" he calls out. There's a moment of embarrassed silence—"what do we do now?" seems to reverberate through the train. Then a man standing near me says, in an equally loud and clear voice, "Thank you!"

As he gets off the train, the Native man offers one last comment: "The creator will be proud of all of you!"

As the train moves on, it seems to float momentarily, and we who have been so generously blessed smile at one other, eyes holding a moment, as though we're old friends, and I think about how much easier it is to see the strands our lives are built on when the quiet of a morning is broken by a leap and a blessing.

LURCHING MAN

THE MAN ON the street was wearing a Hawaiian shirt: white background, red flowers. He was yelling at a man and woman who were passing in front of the door I'd just stepped out of. The couple looked sleek and clean. They wore dark tailored coats, and the woman's hair swung as she turned quickly to look back at the man and then forward again at her mate, who was hurrying along beside her. I couldn't catch what they were saying. I had just stepped into the street myself, so their passing was more of an impression than a scene. The yelling man's words were clear: "Fucking yuppies," he yelled. "Fucking fuck." He turned and walked in the direction I had to go, muttering to himself. He was far enough ahead that if I walked slowly I might not catch up to him, but if I stayed on that street, I knew meeting him would be inevitable—as if there were a string, long and slightly elastic, pulling me into his orbit.

I had just come out of the Shebeen, a tiny pub in Gastown, where I had attended a friend's literary book launch. (Elegant words, friendly company. Add alcohol and stir.) I'd given a little speech at the launch, which had made me excessively nervous, so I'd gulped at my beer afterward as if it were ointment that could settle inflamed thoughts, create ease, turn me into a person I will never be. It didn't work exactly, but there on the street, even though it was Vancouver's infamous Downtown Eastside, and it was night, and many people I knew thought of it as a place of such darkness that once one entered, one might never get out again, I felt comfortable. I'd had the beer, and I'd spent enough time there in daylight to know that the dangers, if any, were more inside myself than out, and that these were more likely to threaten me in other settings. Still, it was night. I'm a woman. The street was dark and my mind busy with its usual tensions.

I soon caught up to the man. As I overtook him, he stopped gesticulating and muttering, looked me in the eye and said hello. I said hello back. He wasn't a big man. His hair was dark and trimmed, so aside from the swearing and the shirt, which stood out mostly because it was winter and not because there was anything especially strange about it, he looked much like anybody. He said, "It's a weird night out here," and I said, "I know," and hoped that would be the end of it. Sometimes people just need the courtesy of acknowledgement, I told myself smugly, comparing myself to the angry couple. I kept walking, and he walked behind me, muttering and cursing again, but not at me, I was pretty sure. We were approaching a busy intersection, a place where the road curves and cars speed around it as if their drivers think they're in the Indy or are afraid of getting caught at a stoplight in the Downtown Eastside.

I stopped a few feet from the curb, and the man continued past me without slowing. A car sped toward us, about half a block away on the inside lane. "Whoa!" I yelled at the man, and "Whoa!" again as he hovered between a lurch forward and a lurch back, inches from the street. His eyes were steady on mine, but not focused, as if I'd interrupted him mid-thought and he was still swimming back from it. I was terrified he'd step out in front of the speeding car, so I opened my mouth and hoped words would come. "You're all right," I managed, trying to project confidence and at the same time wondering why I'd used those words. Whenever my husband says them to me, I usually answer, "How can you tell me I'm all right, and what do you know?" But this man didn't argue. His body grew quieter and he stared at me as if I knew what I was talking about, as if, in fact, I'd given him some necessary information. Then I wondered if my husband had always intended the words as a comfort, not an assumption.

Was I understanding this for the first time? The man stayed there on the edge of the curb, cars rushed past, the light stayed red. At a break in traffic, but still against the light, he lurched across the street and seemed to disappear into the darkness on the other side.

After he was gone I went back to thinking about the launch and my friend and the things I would do tomorrow and tomorrow after that. But when the light changed and I crossed the wide street and saw the man leaning in the shadows against a building, I knew he was waiting for me.

"What's yer name?" the man said as I got closer to him. I didn't answer. He said it again. I turned my head and shook it "no," worried he'd take offence, but not wanting to give away something so personal. My beer brave was wearing thin. I imagined him using my name the way bullies did when I was young, or my mother, when she was disappointed in me. What if he found the right cadence to make me think in some way I owed him?

"You're not going to give me your name?" he said, sounding nonplussed. I stopped and shrugged. Could I even explain it without feeling small? Then he nodded, and I realized that I had liked him right from the start—maybe his inappropriate shirt and the sleekness of the people he had been yelling at, maybe the slightly submissive posture of his body and the reedy sound of his voice. Did he remind me of someone I knew? Or was he just some manifestation of self out there lurching through the world? We both started walking again, him keeping pace, but far off to my left. He called me "ma'am." Told me he'd had a bad night and just wanted to get out of there, go home. I said I understood. By that time we were in a stretch where there were hunched shadows against the buildings, and the light was especially dim. He walked past the shadows with me, then said, "I just need a twenty to get on the bus."

A twenty? I thought, feeling disappointed, or just stupid. What had I expected? "I don't have any money," I told him.

"You don't have a toonie?" He sounded incredulous. His voice went high at the end.

"Oh, a toonie. I thought you said twenty. I don't have twenty." I opened my wallet. He drew nearer. I handed him a five. "Here, get a coffee. Go home," I said speaking the way I had at the curb, like a mother, speaking as if I had any business telling him what to do.

"Thank you, ma'am. God bless," he said. "If you're ever here again and need help, I'm here for you."

I smiled, my idea of the relationship restored, and said goodbye. Just before the SkyTrain station, in a section of exceptional darkness, I saw a man bent in apparent agony. Some force twisting his body, and I wondered, in this new Florence Nightingale view of myself, knowing what to say and all, what on earth could I say to him? I worried that he would fall against me or suddenly rear up. I walked faster. Near the station, an old man sitting in the shrubbery called out as I passed, "Can you spare some change?" I walked past and said nothing, the way I so frequently do.

NATTY MAN

A MAN I KNOW SLIGHTLY rides past our house on his bicycle going uphill. He looks natty in his two-tone jacket and tight black pants. His fifties-style bicycle completes the look, which is self-conscious but well done. Our hill is steep—at the point where gravity and the man's efforts are equally matched, the front wheel wobbles before surging up again. On another person this moment of hesitation could look like waywardness, but on him, a man who pronounces judgments on things without considering the options, the wobble looks more like a flourish.

It's one of those fall days when the air feels like a kiss. The children's voices rise up and down behind me filled with happy notes; occasionally one of them appears, eyes lit with some idea, and the odd leaf makes its way to the ground. I'm sitting on the porch feeling lucky about all this—air, children, leaves—when a single word (Yes!) bursts out from the quiet somewhere high up on the hill. I can't see who's made this word because the view is blocked by trees; it's a man's voice and at first I assume the word will be followed by other words in another voice. But there are none. I am still looking in the direction of the sound because it is that sort of day; I have nothing really to do, and I'm enjoying the last bit of light sunny air when the natty man reappears. This time he's going downhill, and he's taken his jacket off. The jacket's nowhere to be seen, in fact, and I remember that he had glasses on the first time, and now they also are gone. He's going down our hill, and he's apparently just finished talking to himself. There's a look of satisfaction on his face, as though the conversation couldn't be more complete: all sides considered, weighed, and decided upon. As he passes, I wonder would he mind that I have witnessed this moment, and then I think of times when the conversation in my head has suddenly burst forth and I've heard myself talking out loud. The man passes down the street, the children play in the room above me, and I think of all of us in our barely contained worlds and wonder how we manage this every day, keeping it so tamped down and quiet. How do we do that?

PRAYING WOMEN

I AM IN A COFFEE SHOP in Vancouver with my laptop and a friend. We do this once a week, meet across a wooden table and write. My friend writes more than I do. I read, I edit, I write a line, repeat all of the above. On the days I manage to write, it feels as if I've found something—a wisp, a current of air, thin as smoke, that if I look at too closely will disappear. Books about writing offer all manner of helpful advice on how to catch hold of these wisps. In my classes I read out the best ones and feel hopeful and sort of soaring as I do, but when I sit down to write myself, more often than anything else, I flail. Perhaps my teaching should be reduced to two sentences: Flail. Flail some more. I am flailing pretty badly when two young women walk into the coffee shop. The first moves quickly to a table for two at the back, puts her purse over the chair, then walks back to the second woman, who is moving slowly in a sideways sort of direction. The first woman's rushing makes me think of a little dog that runs on ahead and then runs back to make sure you're still following. I decide she is possibly a caregiver and go back to my computer screen.

"The body is our general medium for having a world," I read. This is Maurice Merleau-Ponty in *Phenomenology of Perception*, which I'm looking at because I'm avoiding writing and also because I'm interested in what he has to say about bodies and minds. Does the thought come from what I'm doing, or do I think the thought first and then do it? I watch the two women settle in their chairs and then turn my attention back to the screen.

"My mother and I have the same temperament, but my sister was the black sheep," says a loud voice in the room. There's some kind of murmuring reply, and then more. I'm trying not to listen, but the voices are so loud they insist themselves into my ears. I look over and see that it's the quick-moving woman talking. Her face is a pale oval, topped by a mass of black curly hair. She's like a Modigliani, long-necked and graceful. The other woman replies in a staccato rhythm, equally loud, but halting, like her walk: the words come out, stop, come out again. I go back to my reading, thinking one flaw of the body is that we don't have lids on our ears the way we do on our eyes.

The women talk about how all societies are either being damaged or causing damage. Because I am trying to maintain my composure, I imagine good things, like how wonderful to be so certain, to put a stamp of words around a thing and then move on, as if that is all that has to be said, and that the thought can rest there, undisturbed and undisturbing. The conversation moves to drugs and the wrongness of them, something about a sister, I believe, and then the beautiful one pauses a moment and asks, in the same ringing tones: "I wanted to talk to you about your accident, about what happened after, in the recovery period. What was that like?"

"Well, I was in a coma for eleven days," the slow-moving woman says, speaking clearly this time, with no hesitations. My friend and I look at one another. Sarah Burke, the champion freestyle skier, has very recently died of a head injury. Her story and the word "coma" were in the headlines for weeks. I'm surprised no one else in the café has reacted. The woman's words have come out so clearly, and seemed so stunning, like an announcement. I say quietly, "Are you getting this down?"

"Should we?" my friend whispers.

"And what was that like, could you hear things?" the beautiful woman continues.

"I could hear and I could smell things."

"Really? Like wow. I didn't know that. And then when you woke up, what was that like? What did you feel?"

The questions keep coming. More and more. I can't keep up. Besides, I'm uncomfortable. I recommend this very thing to creative writing students—blithely, it seems now—advising them to go out into the world and copy down other people's words so they can get the feel of real dialogue. When I'm actually doing it, it feels vaguely criminal. Still, behind all that, the hurt woman's grace, her slow, patient answers, and the other woman's nervousness play back and forth across the room.

God is mentioned. And boyfriends and attractiveness, and how some men are attractive but their personalities aren't, and the beauty says she never goes out with a man for more than eighteen months. "I'm a honeymoon person," she says. "I like things at the beginning, and then I get bored."

"Really?" the hurt woman says, sounding shocked.

"I know, I know it's bad," the beauty says. "I know it's something wrong with me." I look up again at that—thinking she's just said something true. Her questions have a tinge of desperation about them, her voice high and a little thin. I get the sense the women don't know each other well, and that the beauty sees the hurt woman as someone who could help her.

More questions. She was different before the accident, she says, yes. "But how?" What's different?"

"Well, when you wake up from a coma you know less," the hurt woman answers. Again I think she's said something so shocking and profound that everyone in the room should be looking up, but no one does. The next words are indistinct until the hurt woman says, "I don't remember. Maybe less patient."

"So your personality changed because you were glad to be alive?"

"I suppose."

"So, I can see how you'd be hard to be with," the beauty says, unaware, it seems, of how this could be taken as an insult.

The talk returns to relationships and then looks. The hurt one says, "But you're very attractive," and the beauty answers, "That's the way God made us, to be attracted to someone because of looks, but then. . ." The rest of her words fall into other sounds in the room until one of them says, "God's great that way, isn't he?"

I try to block them out for a while after that and succeed a little. Other people come in and there are interruptions; though I note more about God and then something about men being limited to only a few personality types, which I think unfair, and then the women's voices drop to a murmur, so I look to see what has finally made them suddenly quiet.

Their heads are bowed, their hands folded together on the table in front of them, and the murmuring sound is coming from the two of them together. Their hands make me think of a time long ago when my daughter had a sweatshirt with a pocket in front. She had put her hands in and wiggled them around. "What are you doing?" I asked. "My hands are having a meeting," she said. Her shirt bumped about wildly. She grinned. "Now they're having an argument."

My friend looks up. "They're praying," I say. "I thought so," she says, her tone happy and her words clipped off at the ends as if she doesn't want to waste any more air on them. "Can I look?" She turns and studies them, turns back. We go back to our typing.

The women pray, and then they talk about groceries, and a moment later they get up, and again, the beauty is quick, and the hurt woman slow. She pushes her chair back and makes sideways, halting progress towards a step down from the raised dais the tables are on. She's a little rounded, her body swathed in sweaters and baggy, shapeless pants. She pauses, choosing which leg to step down with, and then continues her sideways and forward movement. The beauty, with her flowing scarf, rich curls, and pale oval face, moves behind, fluidly, respectfully. I had sensed her nervousness across the room, and now, watching the hurt woman move, I sense her hurt.

In the nineties scientists discovered mirror neurons. These are the neurons in our brains that help us learn. They fire when we watch someone else move. If you throw a ball, your motor neurons fire, explains Vilayanur Ramachandran in a TED talk. If you watch someone else throw a ball, a subset of these neurons fires. It's as if you run a sort of "virtual reality of what you're watching." This is how we can imitate another's movements so quickly, and it's also how we can feel, sometimes, another person's pain. Ramachandran jokingly calls them our "Ghandi neurons." Some people have this to such an extreme they actually feel others' physical pain in their own bodies.

I am not that sensitive, but I do feel a visceral reaction when I watch the hurt woman. Maybe it's an echo of my own accident from deep in my bones, or maybe it's an inherited trait. Sometimes my father, watching news about some disaster, would flinch and say in a voice thick with sympathy, "Oh, those poor people."

My friend closes her laptop. We agree it's time to go. We talk about the women. "They were like a pair of perfectly matched puzzle pieces," she says. "The one injured so badly on the outside, the other on the inside. It was incredible." I agree, thinking about how we find each other, the people we need or care about, and wonder how we do that. Is it more through our bodies or our minds?

Merleau-Ponty was the first philosopher to say we cannot separate the mind and the body. "Inside and outside are inseparable," he said, noting that when we think about an object we give ourselves over to it, "we merge into this body which is better informed than we are about the world . . ."

My friend and I walk outside and go, or merge, into the rest of our days.

SEMANTICS

A FEW YEARS AGO, I went to a retreat centre that a friend had recommended. My friend, a long-lapsed Catholic, assured me that religion wasn't a prerequisite, so I didn't worry about my own state of lapsedness and booked a few days there. On arrival, the minister in charge welcomed me. He was soft-spoken and asked gentle questions, mostly to do with how long would I stay and how was my journey there, but then he asked me what church I attended. I said, "None," and thought I saw a small hardness pass behind his eyes.

Later, he and his wife asked if I could please help them fold some sheets. Afterward they invited me into their suite, where they gave me some juice. The man's wife was rounded and smiling and kind. She told me about living in India, where neighbours would call to one another through the apartment walls and there was a lot of noise and busyness and company all the time. She missed it, she said, and, as she was talking, I missed it too, though I have never lived there, and I haven't lived with neighbours calling to me since I was a child. I used to be sad a lot more often than I am now, and at that time I was sad, and so her kindness felt like an enveloping warmth. I felt accepted, not outside of their circle. Her husband, who was pacing the room, asked, "If you don't go to church, what do you do?" He sounded genuinely perplexed, so I didn't feel defensive, exactly, just uncertain. What do I do? And is there a way to describe it?

I didn't go to the retreat centre again for a few years. I worried that maybe what I was doing there was wrong—not being Christian, that is. That thinking and being quiet and writing, feeling sometimes sad, but also happy to be alone and outside of my regular life, didn't fit the retreat's stated purpose of "spiritual renewal." Time passed, and I reasoned my doubts away, and this time a friend, Fiona, came with me.

After dinner, Fiona went to her room, and I stayed in the kitchen to make myself tea. A woman came in. I'd seen her before, but some people were there on a silent retreat, so I didn't greet her other than to smile. "Hello," she said, and I answered with my own hello, a little disappointed, because I'd been on a silent retreat myself once long ago, and had been looking forward to that satisfying mode of nonverbal communication—a few smiles, the odd gesture, a nod of the head and you're done.

"How much longer are you staying?" she asked.

"Another day."

"You're lucky. I have to leave tomorrow."

I said something like "all good things come to an end" and regretted it, being a cliché, but I was not able to think of anything better.

She opened the fridge door and put her head inside. "We won't be able to say that in eternity."

"Right," I answered, wondering if I'd heard her correctly. She pulled her head out of the fridge and looked at me. "Because they won't come to an end," she said. "They'll just go on and on." She was smiling. She had her food on the counter now and was half turned toward me. She looked happy, and she probably was, and I was happy too, but uncertain now because I wanted to say, "Why can't good things just go on now?" I didn't want to argue with her, even though I felt in a small way that her remark was denigrating my immediate pleasure in tea and my book and solitude, and I suppose in a rather larger way I was denigrating her pleasure in imagining a future of total bliss. Probably she saw my thoughts on my face because her smile faded a little. I made some kind of noncommittal remark, and asked how long she'd been there and would she have a long journey home, and she answered, and so our conversation ended safely and pleasantly enough, but I went back to my room thinking about words and how we use them.

When I studied Aikido, at the beginning of every class we would meditate briefly and then bow to a picture of a gentle-looking man with a white beard and soft eyes. "That's the founder," the teacher had said in our introductory class. "If it makes you uncomfortable to bow to a picture, imagine you are bowing to the best part of yourself." At that point in my life, the best part of myself was pretty invisible to me—and still is, really, so it was a strange thing to think. But even stranger was the fact that "Thou shalt not worship false idols" had sounded loudly in my mind when the teacher had first suggested it, followed by a brief worry that I might be entering some kind of cult. As it turned out, we would bow throughout Aikido class. We would bow to Sensei every time he taught us something, we would bow to one another before and after we began practising, and when I went to Japan I would bow almost every time I looked at someone. I came to like bowing. I came to think of it as a neat and tidy gesture. When a much older woman bowed all the way down to the floor in front of me (after I'd given her a small gift), I felt so humbled and awed by her seemingly complete and graceful obliteration of self that I folded down too. Later, I would realize that I must have made some kind of mistake because you should always bow lower than the person who is bowing to you. This woman couldn't have gone any lower unless she'd somehow been absorbed by the floor.

At the end of our stay, my friend and I were starting our walk down the hill, me with the pack on my back and my computer bag in my hand, Fiona dragging her little wheeled suitcase. We were feeling the weight of all this, the long walk ahead, the noise of the suitcase wheels, when someone called out to us. Did we need a ride somewhere? "Yes, please," we said right away, and he took us to his car and then apologized for the mess of it. "You won't believe this, but I actually cleaned this out, I mean really cleaned it, just a couple of days ago." We chuckled and both of us said innocuous, understanding sorts of things, and then we got in the car, Fiona in the front, me in the back, and we started down the steep hill to the ferry. Fiona made polite conversation, and I looked out the window at the hill falling away beneath us and the curve of the mountains in the distance. I heard him tell her he was about to go to Eastern Europe to run a church there for a few months. "I may stay longer," he said, "if the Lord wants me to." At first I thought he was mentioning someone's name, and it took me a moment to realize he was talking about God. "Do you speak the language?" Fiona asked, and he said no, and that it was going to be a problem possibly.

"Are you going to learn?"

"I'm going to have to pray about that," he said.

"Why not just take lessons or get a book?" leapt into my mind, but fortunately didn't leap out of my mouth. He was a nice young man, as my mother would have said. Kind and well-mannered. After he dropped us off, Fiona and I talked a little about language: "Lord" and "Eternity," words that had been dropped around us over the past couple of days, and which I had just let lie, where they fell, not knowing what to do with them, not wanting to pick them up under false pretenses.

A few days later, Fiona said we shouldn't have been there, that we didn't belong, not being religious, and I felt deep pangs of guilt, suspecting myself of transgressing something that's sacred—and now transgressing even more as I write about it. "Writers are always selling somebody out," Joan Didion said.

I look up "prayer" on Google, the god in my machine. "Prayer has the characteristics of a deeply meaningful conversation between two people," says one site. "It's communicating with God. It's the practice of the presence of God," says another. I read the retreat literature again, looking for clues to see if I'd transgressed. Years ago, when friends would talk about being lapsed Catholics and after I'd read Joyce's *Portrait of the Artist as a Young Man*, I remember feeling envious. There wasn't much you could say about being a lapsed Anglican except that the Anglican god of my childhood seemed to be someone like Martha Stewart, good at making beds with hospital corners and knowing which fork to use. There was so much drama in a Catholic childhood. There was guilt, sure, but there was also forgiveness. I call up the retreat centre to ask if they mind if atheists come and stay. Good atheists, I want to add, but don't, figuring that the person on the other end of the phone, being a sympathetic person who cares about people's souls, will understand by the way I'm asking that I'm a nice person, a sincere person, and that even though I don't believe in God per se, I do believe in a lot of the same things that they do. The person is lovely. She sounds as though she accepts and has seen and can manage all manner of things, even atheists. "We don't ask people that," she says. "The people who run it are a Christian community but we believe in being open to all. We welcome everyone." I thanked her and booked another retreat. After I hung up, feeling absolved, I realized that that's what I'd been looking for all along.

THE INNER WEED

MY MOTHER HAD A white streak in her hair from her early forties on. It suited her. Gradually the rest of her hair grew in grey to match it, and then, like so many other women of her generation, she went to the hairdresser and had it blued. My hair dulled to a mousy brown as the colour slowly leached out. I used henna to brighten it until finally there was so much grey, my hair turned the colour of a fire hydrant or a maple leaf in fall. I relented, let the grey come in. My husband insisted he found grey sexy, which, by comparison to looking like Howdy Doody, I suppose it was. Still, I found it dull. I decided to go to the hairdresser and have her add some white streaks. I wanted some drama, some brightness, something.

The hairdresser put a cap on my head and started pulling hairs through the holes in it with a little spike, which supposedly had a blunt end, but looked like a gaffing tool. I tried not to wince, not because I'm brave or tough, but because I have absorbed the lessons of my childhood, which were not to show your fear, not to cry when you were hurt, and not to be sensitive or weedy—a word that either I adopted during an intense period of *Coronation Street* watching in my twenties or that's leaked out from some strand in my DNA. In the Oxford dictionary, weedy means "thin and physically weak," but in my interpretation it also means weak-minded and possibly tubercular. I know this is overly dramatic. And it definitely doesn't fit with the ethos of my mother's family, who came from England some generations ago and helped to settle the North, but still follow so many of their ancestors' habits, I think I recognize them in the Jane Austen novels I'm addicted to. On special occasions at the cottage, we wore white and ate small sausages in tiny buns. When I moved away from home, I found out that not everyone had to wear white on birthdays, and then only after I had watched a lot of movies about the English in India, I understood the thinking. We in our rattling-down cottages with spiders that crawled over us in the night (sometimes leaving welts as big as golf balls on our stomachs and arms) were meant to carry on the Empire.

When the hairdresser was done with the gaffing hook, she slathered the dye over top, a light and frothy chemical stew, sealed it with plastic and then set me under a hair dryer that looked just like the ones my mother used to sit under forty years ago. Next to the chair was a stack of magazines. I picked up a *Canadian Geographic* and scanned the first few pages, then settled on a short piece about the relative speeds of mice and elephants. Mice, I learned, move as quickly as they do because their body size and nerve size are neatly matched. An elephant, if it were to move as quickly as a mouse, would need nerves as thick as football fields (or 160 feet in diameter, I think they mean); and then would you want elephants moving quickly?

I was recovering from the poking and plucking quite nicely when I became aware of a pressure point on my forehead where the cap was digging in. It was relatively mild at first (as compared, say, to being continually stabbed in the scalp) but soon hurt so much I decided there must be something inside my head that the cap was pressing on, possibly a tumour or an aneurysm, and that it could at any moment burst. *Woman dies for vanity*, I imagined the headline. I wouldn't be the first. As the pain intensified, I pictured a Richter scale for pain, multiplying exponentially once you noticed it, and then chastised myself for being so dramatic. During these sorts of episodes I recognize a high degree of weediness in myself and remember decades earlier when I got up in the night to ask about rustling sounds in the wall near my head. I was sleeping in the top bunk at our cabin. My mother said they were bats and told me to go back to bed. A moment later, thinking about bats so close to me, I heard her say to my father, "I didn't realize Janey was so skittish."

A few years ago, to encourage an attitude of interest rather than fear, I took my daughter to the bug zoo in Victoria. We marvelled together over the stick insects and millipedes in their aquariums, and when a young woman giving a talk on tarantulas asked for a volunteer from the audience, I put my hand up. She eyed me as I walked up to her. She had already explained how fragile spiders are because their skeletons are on the outside of them, not inside, like ours. If it falls, it will die, she said, looking at me fiercely. I thought of my bones, sheltered within the pillowy casing of my body, and felt grateful for this arrangement and sorry for the tarantula's, then sat on the chair and put out my hand. "Hold it flat," she said, "and don't move." The tarantula sat quietly on my open palm. "They're not all that poisonous," she said. "Their bite is not as bad as a wasp's, but if they're frightened, they can shoot out the hairs from their legs, and if these get into your skin they can be extremely painful, and if into your eyes, they can blind you." I sat there with my palm outstretched, concentrating on not moving and hoping both the spider and I could stay unafraid, and I wondered if showing my daughter this was enough, or was there a certain amount of weediness that just gets passed along in your DNA?

Last year our cat died and shortly after, a family of mice moved in. I would see them flitting along the back of the kitchen counter, slipping behind the kettle and the coffee maker, the jug of spoons. They moved as quickly as shadows or floaters drifting (or shooting) across the periphery of my field of vision. I knew it was a family because I'd seen one of the young, a tiny thing, a mere toddler of a mouse slip behind the piano and then under it and out into the middle of the living room, where it froze a moment, in toddler indecision, then turned and went back under the piano. I thought of the article about nerves and elephants, and then the next time I saw one—in the kitchen, popping up through an element in the stove—I thought how much like water they are, silent and slipping. By that point, I had developed an odd sort of fondness for them. They were filling in some of the space left by the cat, who had required frequent feedings at the end of her life and a certain amount of cleaning up after. I set traps baited with cheese or peanut butter. Next day I would steel myself for a body, but the trap would be empty, the food gone. I put poison out in a little saucer and set it on the kitchen windowsill. The poison was bright blue, but it looked like the sugar-coated anise seed candies you get in Indian restaurants. In the morning, the saucer would be empty, and later in the day, scuttling sounds or another shadow slipping across the periphery of my vision.

One morning, the house quiet, the aftermath of everyone's leaving had left a lovely emptiness. I was alone, a state I'm always looking for but not always happy to be in. And then there was a scrabbling sound in the kitchen. At first I tried to believe it was something else, the fridge, the furnace—anything—but it kept happening. I realized it was coming from the basket where we kept bags of dried pasta. I picked up the basket and the sound stopped. I put it down again. Did I really want to be handling a basket of mice? But then I talked myself into it, realizing this was the perfect opportunity to move them out of the house without killing them, much in the way I extract large bees or wasps—trapping them with a glass and a piece of paper, then taking them outside and setting them free. It's not that I won't kill things, it's more that I feel it unfair to murder everything that happens to fly or scuttle into my house. I've even started hesitating before squishing the cereal moths. I study the feelers, so delicate they're almost invisible, then their eyes at the base, like the heads of tiny pins. This is a creature, I think, then squish it against the wall, leaving a grey-brown smear, like dust.

I walked quickly, holding the basket of mice far away from me. I was trying not to think of panicky mice crawling up the sides of the basket and onto my arm. I wasn't feeling brave or resourceful or any of the things that my mother had raised me to be, even though in that moment I was probably doing what she would have done. I wondered briefly if she was scared all those times I thought she was brave. I decided not. She was always brave. And so it struck me that I did a lot of pretending as a mother: pretending I was brave, pretending I knew the answers to questions, and that if at any time my pretending looked like courage, it was because of her example.

The mice in the basket must have been shocked by the movement. They stayed still as I carried them out to the back deck, and were still a moment longer after I put the basket down and then tipped it onto its side with my foot. One mouse ran like a streak straight from the deck into the air, flying straight out, and seeming to hang there for a moment before the weight of its tiny body made it fall in a graceful arc. I marvelled at the beauty of this, a creature suspended momentarily in air, and was about to walk over to see if it was lying stunned on the lower deck, when a second mouse ran straight past me into the house. I yelped and jumped, both feet in the air, just like the weediest women do in the movies.

DUCKS

IT WOULD BE BETTER to write a poem about ducks because no one would know you were talking about your life—your husband, your marriage, your children. You could distract them with the partial slick of ice on the lake, willows on the bank, bullrushes. You could have them think about the conversations they were having—or not having—with their partners, and then you could let them think about love and the way it's always layered with sediment. Your children, your real children, meanwhile, gambol ahead, the sun shines, and the people and the lake and the leaves (falling, red, orange, brown) all chatter together making a sound that could be rustling—or is that peace you're listening to?—a single moment of stillness as you cross the wooden bridge (the stream), and your feet don't slip in the mud on the other side. At first no one notices when the dog rushes your daughter as if she's some kind of game and your daughter runs as if it's some kind of chase. You call at her to stand still but she won't and then there are three dogs, and everyone's running: you, the dogs, your husband. You go to your child, your husband goes to the dogs, and when he kicks at the air around them, a woman yells and he yells back, and in the midst of all that yelling—the stupid, stupid woman with the stupid, stupid dogs—you say one quiet "fuck"; and then you realize it is right beside your daughter's ear and that with one syllable you have just wiped out all those careful years—not saying fuck or shit or goddamn fucking sonafabitch—and because of that and so much more—the arrogance of the woman's neck and the smugness of her feet—the act of kneeling beside your crying child (instead of following the woman and slamming her to the ground) becomes at once the hardest thing you've ever done and a prayer—make me better than I am. All the while, gulls stand on iced over bits of lake and ducks bob in open water.

GRACES

MIMESIS

I N A WORKSHOP with a famous poet, a friend of mine learns that a good story generates tension between the narrative and the lyrical. The narrative goes along the X-axis, the lyrical along the Y-, or the other way round. Too much X and it is flat, too much Y and it doesn't make sense, he explains. This makes writing sound a bit like math, which can be comforting. I like the idea of math, and I like knowing there are people in the world who quantify things that are difficult for me and make lines and angles and numbers out of them.

The other night on the blackboard at the back of the classroom where I teach a writing class, someone from a previous class had drawn a graph illustrating the law of supply and demand, or maybe it was economies of scale, or maybe even the "indifference curve," with one variable represented on the X-axis, the other on the Y-axis. In the space between was one of those perfect rising arcs that makes you think of soft hillsides of waving grasses and sunsets and other hopeful things, not dreary economic conundrums mulled over by men who look like Warren Buffett.

Our topic that night was definition, so we talked about ideas like persistence and family and love and then how we could define them on paper, one way being to set a thing among its fellows in a category and then to find the elements about it that made it unique. As the students wrote I looked at the graph at the back of the room. On the way home I happened upon a radio show about the meaning of beauty, so I drove listening to disembodied voices doing what we had been trying to do in the class, pin down something that shivered and slipped out from under us. I wanted someone to say what it is about beauty that startles us so and hoped they would consider proportion and the golden mean, as one of my students (a mathematician) had done in an essay, and then gone beyond that to consider why humans respond so viscerally to something that can be expressed in numbers. But the moments of beauty the voices ascribed most passion to were acts, not visions: people doing good rather than scenes or images of looking good. Eventually someone used the word "grace," and one man, David Adams Richards actually, said he'd seen people in the deepest poverty show their true selves "without mimicry." Mimicry: I thought mimicry was a kind of party trick, not something behind which we hide our "true selves," but the program ended before I could learn more.

An entry in Wikipedia defines "mimicry" as a perfectly respectable biological survival tactic categorized by a variety of styles. Batesian mimics, for instance, are creatures that assume the coloration of more dangerous relatives to avoid being eaten by predators, and are named for Henry W. Bates, an English naturalist, but I think of Norman Bates from *Psycho* instead and wonder if scientists ever consider the confusion the name might evoke. Or do they amuse themselves by thinking that Norman Bates initially looked harmless, but was actually dangerous, so the name could be a scientific paradox, a little joke in the language. Remember Janet Leigh's scream in the shower and Bates's shadow against the curtain: if she had not been beautiful, would he have bothered to attack her?

Vavilovian mimicry is the name given to weeds that mimic the coloration and shape of the plants they grow among. Nikolai Ivanovich Vavilov was a man who looks at first glance a little like Groucho Marx, and then after closer study, a little like my grandfather, who was born four years before Groucho. This was the late nineteenth century, the moustachioed era, when men grew Fuller brushes under their noses and looked out at cameras as if they were defending themselves from assault. Mullerian and

Mertensian mimicry apply to species that borrow traits from one another to fool others into thinking they're harmless when they're actually dangerous, which is nefarious, if you ask me, and not a little mean-spirited, but scientists don't attribute judgment to their categories, and they don't spend time thinking about the sound "Mertensian mimicry" makes in the mind, but then is it reasonable to divide people into categories: scientists and non-scientists and such, or is that another sort of nefariousness—to imagine oneself fitting neatly into one category and therefore unable or unwilling to consider the usefulness of being the kind of person who can adapt and fit into another?

Last summer my family and I went to the interior of BC to visit relatives. We usually check into a quiet motel filled with other ordinary families like our own, so it's not a time when we feel the need for performance or guardedness of any kind. But this was the May long weekend, a paradigm shift apparently during which the town fills with people excited to be alive and drinking beer. I had booked a motel we'd stayed at before, one of those little places near the lake where the rooms are consecutively numbered units in a long one- or two-storey building that forms a squared-off horseshoe around a parking lot. We have a photo of my husband and daughter in the middle of one of those horseshoes years ago, their bodies surrounded by empty space. Their backs are to the camera and they're walking towards the lake, which shimmers before them. They're holding hands. My daughter, who was two at the time, wears a little blue dress that flares out from her legs. Her hand reaches up to my husband's. You can see in her posture, in the shape her blue dress makes against the sky that this is beauty in its highest form: grace in their fingertips and in the space between them.

When we pulled into this parking lot on this night, we wondered if this truly had been the motel where we'd stayed all those years earlier. A party was in full swing at one end of the lot—a circle of motorcycles, people spilling out an open motel room door. As we got out of the car, two young women walked past us towards the party, their faces already smeared loose with alcohol, their bodies linked at the arm, their voices loud. They were moving in that way you do when you know you're going towards something exciting, possibly sex, and you're still young, and you don't know what that's going to mean to you, but you know you want it, or your body does. Your body is going ahead of you towards the music and the beer and the men and the smoke and the voices jangling out in the night air.

We looked at each other. "Shall we just check out now?" my husband asked. We found a place two doors down with no party going on and a manager who promised she never slept on May long weekends "in order to keep a lid on things," as she put it. There was a group of women on one side of the horseshoe who were yelling happy remarks to one another, and at the end a pod of men, greying and bearded, sat in plastic chairs, their motorcycles parked in front of them. Our room was directly above them. As we walked past, the men didn't look up, and their voices rolled out the syllables companionably among themselves. Outside our door, I paused to listen more closely to them, my radar tuned for talk of parties. "I've paid every month, and I pick them up every weekend, just the way the judge outlined it, so I'm doing my bit," one of the men said. I braced for the response, which I imagined would be bitter and tinged with long-cherished wounds, but the voice was so quiet I couldn't hear it, so I went into the room, and the night settled. We slept undisturbed except for the loud sighs of our teenaged son shifting uncomfortably on his bed.

The next day as my daughter and I walked towards our car, one of the men smiled and said, "Are you here for the soccer tournament?" I said no, but our eyes met in that shared space that soccer parents recognize anywhere. We've stood on the same sidelines in the pounding rain. We've yelled the same words of encouragement to our kids.

We spent the day among family, among the various bits of our criss-crossed DNA, where we enjoyed the new baby among us, wondering whose eyes she had and where she got her delicate limbs, and delighting in the way she communicated with us, her smiles sparking out at us, making us laugh and look at each other with a new line of connection, another rising bit of hope arcing between us.

When we got back to the hotel, the men in the room below were busy packing up their bikes. My husband said, "They're Hells Angels," and I said, "No, they're not. They couldn't be." "They're wearing their colours," he said. I studied them from the safety of our room above, and saw that indeed they were, even the man with the gentle face, who had talked to us of soccer. They called out to one another over the sound of their bikes. One of them commented on an empty house behind the hotel, an attractive place, well proportioned, with large picture windows on either side of the front door, a place I could imagine us living in, filled with space and light. "Look," the Hells Angel said. "We should buy that. It'd be a great place for parties." I couldn't hear the response because they gunned their bikes then, the roar of their engines slamming into us like fists, or declarations.

THE PLOT OF A LIFE

THE DAY MY FATHER DIED, I was preparing a lecture on plot for the introductory creative writing class I teach. My sister and I had already been at his bedside for a number of hours and we agreed to come back in shifts later in the day after taking care of some necessary work. She went to her meeting and I came home to prepare for my class.

At home, I settled down with my books and notes: we had navigated several of these scares before. But not even such writing authorities as John Gardner, E.M. Forster and Anne Lamott could help me now. My father, a man of science and reason, was having trouble breathing, how could I deliver a lesson on plot? For me plot represents a forced injection of rationality into an area I prefer to navigate by instinct. It means come inside and tidy your room, do your homework, brush your teeth, behave. My mother's exhortations, but behind them the example of my father— the heights a person can reach by paying attention to logic and following the rules. I wished I could go back to the lecture on character, in which I'd encouraged the class to explore. Follow every whim, I told them. You never know when you might find gold.

E.M. Forster says in real life: "perfect knowledge of other human beings is an illusion and that is why novels can solace us: they suggest a more comprehensible and thus a more manageable human race, they give us the illusion of perspicacity and power."

When my siblings and I were young, my father would come home from work and sink onto the chesterfield between us, taking our hands in his. "Lights of my life," he'd say, sighing happily. It seemed we were his solace and that we knew and understood him perfectly, our generous and loving father. On weekends he'd retreat to the basement, and the house would reverberate with the soaring notes of an aria or the repetitive staccato of a language tape. He learned French during the war, and later he acquired Spanish, Italian, and smatterings of Portuguese and German. Language seemed to stick to him. He once told me that if he'd followed his inclinations, he would have taught language rather than pathology. At dinner he spoke French to me, Le poivre, mon cheri, and I felt blessed and chosen. Every year when we watched *The Wizard of Oz* together, I thought of it as a golden time—his delight seemingly as rich and deep as ours.

Many years later, when my husband's saxophone quartet played "Over the Rainbow" at our wedding, I smiled at my father, thinking he would recognize this as the tribute I intended. I wanted him to know the soaring optimism I sometimes felt was associated with him: his endless curiosity, empathy, intelligence. He nodded, but more in irritation than recognition, and I felt a familiar wave of defeat. By this time, I was well into my thirties, no longer the light of his life—a dim bulb, perhaps? It was hard for me to tell.

At twenty, I moved west, drawn by my father's romantic descriptions of the land he'd grown up in—snowdrifts so high you could slide down roofs into them, mountains that cast shadows early in the afternoon. I remember feeling disappointed to discover highways and gas stations just like everywhere else. Still, I found pleasure living at Whistler, skiing, climbing, and living on my own. A few years later, I went back to school, my father separated from my mother, and moved into the same building as me. "Darling, you've made me weep," he said when he discovered I'd arranged his furniture for him before he arrived. I remember feeling overwhelmed by his emotion; how could I possibly live up to it?

The years passed—many dinners, my father still my father, never quite stepping away from his lectern, his mind always five steps ahead of mine, his grasp of all things professorial and complete. If I dared refute him, sometimes his response seemed defensive, and I remembered some of the other comments he had made at our family's dinner table: "There's no point letting women into medical school when they're just going to have babies and leave," he said; and "Being a secretary is a fine thing for an intelligent woman to do," and finally: "You can always tell a woman's age by her neck."

People say there are conversations you must have with your parents before they die—I love you, I forgive you. We managed only half. "I'm done," he said a few weeks before his death. "Done breakfast?" I asked, though I knew he wasn't really referring to the toast in front of him. "I've had enough." His voice was firm and loud, and he glared at me through his bleary eyes. We were alone in his room. I had come back to visit early after a night thinking it was time to phone all the siblings. "Make sure he's propped up on his pillows," I'd said to the aide the night before. "Don't let him drown in his sleep."

"I love you," he said a few minutes later when I helped him settle onto his bed. "I love you, too," I replied. But there was wariness in both our voices. At one point while I was still in university, he had wanted me to move in with him. When I refused, my mother intervened to explain he couldn't expect that from me. "I don't know what I'd do without you," he used to say after I helped him through another hospital stay; half an hour later he'd accuse me of stealing something from his room.

On the morning of the day he died, my father held my sister's hand and looked lovingly into her eyes. She, who had become part of his life much later, had succeeded where I hadn't, becoming a friend and confidante over the last difficult year and a half. He stared at me for a long while after she left—silent, as he had been all morning. When I got up to tell him I would return in the afternoon, I adjusted my scarf. His last words, delivered to me alone, were rasping, pained and irritated: "Take that thing off your neck," he said.

John Gardner says that a sequence of causally related events can end either in resolution or in logical exhaustion, a recognition that we've reached the stage of infinite repetition—more events will follow, but they will all express the same thing.

My father died at about three o'clock that afternoon. He died alone—frightened, perhaps, or maybe just relieved. When I arrived a few minutes later, the cleaning woman offered me tea and her shoulder to cry on.

My class on plot, deferred until after my sister and I took care of the necessary endings, was fractured. Structure is something that takes care of itself if you're paying attention, I might have told them. Listen to your characters, I hope I added.

Now that my father has died, the facts of his life are still and quiet, and my instincts are confirmed. I do not derive much meaning from the plot of his life—what I look for are the tendrils of his character that have seeped into me. When I write fiction, occasionally a character speaks stingingly, in a whip of words, and I feel myself braced and awakened. It seems to me that this is my father speaking—and now, with death between us, any word from him is welcome.

APPLES

OUTSIDE MY WINDOW there are apples, small and perfect, glowing pink and yellow. Another two weeks and they'll be fully red and ready. They hang there, a picture of bounty. Richness. Jewelled fruit. I imagine picking them, relieving the tree, the apples falling into the bowl, one against the other with small thuds.

Next door the neighbour's child chatters in his kitchen. He will come outside soon. There will be noise. That's a title. There will be noise. I sit in my messy office in the backyard imagining that my mind will get clear enough for words to come into it, all the while the clatter of dishes, the buzz of a saw at another neighbour's renovation down the street. The neighbour's child is cute, five years old, with a grin that opens the world, just there, and you'd be a fool not to see it. He will be out in the yard soon and then his mother will be out after him, calling for him to be careful.

My sister and I took our father's ashes up to Mount Revelstoke where the air is sharp and smells like trees and lichen and the flowers are so bright and everything feels like wonder, and yet we worried where to put him, where we could feel the import of what we were doing. We walked up to the fire tower where we thought he had worked when he was sixteen. At least I thought he had. I remembered him talking about it at the dinner table, the loneliness of it, and the beauty. You get to this mountain park by driving up a long road with many switchbacks. It's a national park. I'm saying this because my father's father was mayor of Revelstoke when the road was built. So we took our father up his father's road and then to the fire tower where he'd worked at sixteen and we left him there. Was that cruel?

He'd been in my cupboard for ten years. Long enough. I would go looking for the Hallowe'en decorations and find him, a shock sometimes. Do we realize how deep in our bones our parents are? I don't want my children to. I want them to take me for granted. And later, I want them to know that they'll survive their grief, and that I'll still be there after I'm gone. That actually, even if they want to, they won't be able to get rid of me because they'll keep recognizing me in themselves, in something they do with their hands, or an expression they use, or in the way they see light and exclaim over it.

We walked around the fire tower and took pictures, and we asked a woman to take a picture of the two of us, and then we found a small path that petered out above rocks and scrub brush, and we looked around to be sure there were no people who could see us. "Here?" my sister asked, and I said, sure. She opened the canister and shook it in big jerking movements so the ashes came out quickly, in clumps. With my mother's ashes, we had passed the bag among us carefully, shaking small bits of her into the lake, as if we were adding salt to soup, and then we passed it on to the next person, the bag passing between us several times. My sister flung our father, like she was baking a grand pie, a pie for the gods. Here, she should have called. "Take him!" But she didn't. She was silent and firm and excessive, and afterwards there were ashes on her feet.

When I said, "Can I have some, please?" my sister answered, "Oh, there's lots here," with an emphasis on "lots," and then handed the canister to me. It was almost empty. I don't want you to think I minded. I'd had him in my cupboard all those years. Keeping him to myself. He'd registered with the memorial society and had given instructions for them to take care of his ashes themselves. He was like that. Not wanting to "burden" us, as he would have put it. I thought of that, his separateness, as I poured the last of him out. Then knelt down and touched the ash on the rock, spread it with my fingers, fine dust, the colour of granite. Our bones. Dust. I brushed some of the dust from my sister's feet. I read Mary Oliver's poem "Sleeping in the Darkness" because I thought he'd like to be in the company of insects and birds and dark. "All night I heard the small kingdoms/ breathing around me, the insects/ and the birds who do their work in the darkness." My voice shook with my reading-out-loud nerves even though it was just my sister there, and then I gave her Seamus Heaney's "A Kite for Michael and Christopher" because I thought we should give my father's boyhood back to him, the happy times with the sister he loved and the wild air of mountains. "Before the kite plunges down into the wood/ and this line goes useless/ take in your two hands, boys, and feel/ the strumming, rooted, long-tailed pull of grief." She read clearly and well, her voice not shaking. And then we walked back to the path and down again to where there is a small pond. "I'm going to rinse the bag here," I said, thinking of my father's ashes on the ends of my fingers where I'd touched him, touched the lichen and the rock underneath.

My neighbour's door opens and the child emerges, a small explosion spilling out into the world. "Oh my god, oh my god, oh my god," he chants as he runs. "Dawson," his mother calls, her voice following him like the tail of a kite. "Come inside. You can't go on the swing in your bare feet." He ignores her, the happy thud of his bare feet free on wet grass.

FISH

The heart has reasons which reason doesn't know.

— Pascal

I START WITH THE FISH, where it always begins, or ends, I'm not sure that matters. Maybe fish is where we were, or what we were at the beginning. Swimming. Cold-blooded with scales and guts like pearls, gills folding in and out like accordions or fans and my siblings there and my mother, the boat nothing to brag about, a small outboard, big enough for the three or four of us who went out every night after dinner, the lake quiet or the lake heaving up and down under us and our boat riding its surface like a slap, the edges of waves like cliffs, nothing but air underneath and my fear the boat would break or the next wave would flood over, and there we'd be inside the lake, the lake inside of us.

There were two places our mother liked to fish—opposite the pump house near the point and a place in Sandy Bay where we swam in the afternoons. We would line ourselves up with an oak on the shore. "There's a hole down there," our mother told us. "That's where the fish live." I would think of the fish below us swimming in or out of their hole as we sat above on the hard seats of the boat, casting our lines, waiting for them, watching the ash of our mother's cigarette grow longer and longer. We talked about lures and complained about the orange keyhole life jackets that she made us wear. They stank of must and were too tight when we pulled them over our heads. They made us feel like accident victims with neck collars.

If one of us caught something, there'd be the excitement of the fish dancing above the water, leaping and pulling and fighting and then the flurry with the net, dipping the loop of metal down below the fish and quick, quick scooping it up. Inside the boat, the fish would curl and smack the floor in hurried beats, sometimes flipping so high there was the danger of it getting out. I would draw my legs up close, afraid of being stabbed by a fin, afraid of the chaos of something so fiercely alive, always glad when my mother smashed it on the head with a rock, and it would lie still, dead and safe.

If it wasn't too late when we got back, our mother let us watch her clean the fish on the kitchen counter. They were supple and silvery against the stained yellow tiles, and the rough plywood edge pressed into the flesh of our arms as we perched on chairs, bent close, watching. The knife our mother used, with its stained blade, cut surely into the flesh, first a slice behind the gills to remove the head. Then the shiver of blade into belly, soft and pale, where jewels appeared, and the curl of fish gut spilled out onto our counter like a pale worm. There were other masses, yellow and bluish grey, small indistinct shapes, and sometimes there were eggs, a sac of perfect translucent circles, but mostly not. What we all loved best: the dark red wedge of liver and the story our mother told, her voice lifting over the syllables, the knife still separating pale fish flesh from bone—about the time my sister popped a liver in her mouth and swallowed it.

When I was a little older, after summer camp and sailing lessons, my mother and aunts bought a boat, and then my mother would take me out with her. She didn't like to sail the quiet side of the bay next to the breakwater, but would head straight into the wind and tack through the narrow gap that was closest to our dock.

She would sail the boat so close to the rocks I could see the flecks of quartz in the boulders, could see the mass of them rising up in the water below us. We'd be less than a foot from one of these knife edges, and I'd have the paddle raised, ready to fend us off, when she'd calmly say, "ready about," and the bow would swing, smooth as a golf club slicing air, and I'd have to scramble quick to the other side and haul in the jib quick as I could so as not to lose any wind.

The next tack would take us to the boulders on the other side of the gap. I had walked out there in my bare feet, it was known territory, but I knew in the deep water beside the boulders there were pike, long-bodied fish with teeth, waiting.

One more tack, and we'd slide just a hair past the rocks, the wind and wave coming on like a train, and I would climb fast to my spot near the bow, where I'd hike out, turn and look at my mum, she'd grin, and we'd be away.

The day of my wedding my mother asked me to go for a walk. In the TV movies, this is the point when the mother gives the daughter helpful tips or tells stories about her romantic life with the woman's father. We walked. I pointed out the willows next to the lake and told her that some mornings I would see red-winged blackbirds there. She nodded, but was otherwise silent, and I remembered she was always quiet on walks. Over the years we had taken many, and I had talked a little, and she had nodded in agreement or said something about the leaves or the weather and then was silent again. I hope that on this walk she knew that when I mentioned the blackbirds and the willows that I was saying that I had liked my childhood and was grateful to her. We walked around twice and then came back to the house. And then I got married.

On a camping trip, my daughter lost a silver ring that had been my grandmother's. She had been swimming in a small lake where she and her friend had been playing on a log. My sister had given the ring to my daughter while we were visiting just a few weeks earlier. "Dive," I told her, shocking myself with the note of command in my voice.

"I tried," my daughter said. "I tried twice."

"Try again."

"It's just a ring," she said, using her teenager voice, the one that covers over the places where it hurts.

I swam over to the girls and held on to the end of the log. "Where?" They pointed. I dove and felt the immediate inadequacy of my arms and limbs. I was only a few feet beneath the surface and already in another world. It was like entering Mordor itself; beneath was the infinite unknown, green and only slightly glowing, filled with particles, the water almost viscous. It would be darker and darker below, perhaps forever. Not even the sun could get to it, so how could I dare? I imagined creatures down there or logs, thick with slime that would feel like arms curling around me, malevolence reaching up. I surfaced, dove one more time, but couldn't force myself down any farther. "It's just a ring," my daughter repeated. I swam back to the dock, where I pulled myself out into the warmth and thought of the time, long after my grandmother had died, when I had dreamt that she appeared beside my bed in my little apartment in Victoria. I had just started a new life and was feeling starkly alone and unsure of myself. In the dream she spoke as clearly as if she were alive and real. "You're doing well," she said. "I'm proud of you."

Last summer I visited my older sister at a small cottage on an island not far from where our cottage used to be. The air smells the same there, and the lake and the bushes and the grass make the same sounds, the small laps and tickles of water on rock, the small shufflings and rustles of animals in the bushes. I took my sister's kayak and paddled out into the shallow bay to look at the remains of old ships sunk there when the island was used for shipbuilding. The ribs sit a foot or two below the surface, and they glow a little in the water, lit by sunlight. They're green, softened by algae, and they curve down into the dark. Paddling over top of them, I worried about hitting one and unbalancing, tipping into the water and then knocking myself against those hard surfaces; then after floating there a few more moments a more atavistic fear got hold of me. I felt as if the ribs of the old ships below me were ghosts, and the ribs were the outstretched fingers of the dead reaching for unwitting people foolish enough to get close, like the trigger hairs of flesh-eating plants just waiting for something warm and breathing to come near. No matter how much I told myself it was irrational, my fear wouldn't subside. I paddled quickly back closer to shore where there were just rocks below and reeds and wondered where this fear had come from. Why so powerful?

When my mother died, we took her ashes out in the lake. On a calm, windless day, we rowed an old aluminum boat through the gap to a spot thirty feet off a point on the shore where there used to be an old lighthouse. The lighthouse was small, painted red and white, with a single rotating light. We used to clamber at its base sometimes. It gave us a sense of importance, thinking of boats in the night, and the beacon shining out to them.

My sister and I were in the boat with our two aunts. Our brother and younger sister were not with us, though they knew of our plans. We rowed until we could see the elm behind the lighthouse where our grandmother's and one of our great aunt's ashes are, and then we stopped.

My aunt recited a poem, and we passed the ashes from one to the other, each of us pouring a little of my mother into the lake. The fine grey particles of her spread out in the clear water like a small cloud. We passed the bag around a few times. On the second time, I didn't take it properly from my sister, and some of the ashes spilled into the boat. "Oh!" my sister said in exactly the same tone as our mother would have used. I took the bag again and poured a little more. After we returned to shore and others had joined us for a sherry on the lawn of our grandmother's cottage, I took the whisk and dustpan to the boat. I was in the bay where our dock used to be, where we had hauled boats out of the water at the end of the season, stepping tentatively into the water where there were leeches and the bottom was thick with a fine silky muck that would rise up around our ankles, black and stinking. Behind me the scrubby brush, the small stones, and the dirt where we used to dig for worms. I rinsed the bits of ash off the dustpan and thought how ordinary this small task, how plain this spot, how cool the water on my hands.

REMAINS

I VISIT THE LAND in winter where the lake has thrown ice at the shore, long shattering tendrils that pull the branches down, like slow tears in ice and wood. I take pictures: the trees, the shore, my aunt—a small rounded figure in an old ski jacket and stained wool pants. I feel the years shared, the ghosts in the air as my bones, the swing of my arms and legs part of the labyrinth of compensation and reward my brain has become: the land, my aunt, me—no difference.

The space where the cottage used to be is a small emptiness. I stand where my bedroom once was and think pink walls, two windows, the sound of waves lapping against the shore. At the fence by the guide camp, my aunt pulls her eighty-three-year-old body up and gets stuck with one leg half over, like a young, awkward girl. I guide her down, worrying over broken things, my family incredulous—*You couldn't keep her from climbing? What were you thinking, letting her near there?* My aunt finds a different route to the shore, studies a snake skin, the skeletal remains of leaves. I think of the day she pulled a dead gull from the lake by its head, the body falling away as she lifted it, how gently she had placed the head on the beach, then eased the rest of the corpse in by a wing—feather and bone slipping through water.

LEAH

O UR BEDSPREAD IS BROWN. This is a mistake. It looks like
marmite. I don't even like marmite. As well as that, it's new and
slightly shiny, but wrinkled and dotted with bits of fluff. The fluff is
especially offensive, or maybe it's the shine. Bedding should not shine.
Our dressers, not matching, are covered with sad things: bits of papers,
mismatched or never-worn earrings, ticket stubs, a small carving of a water
buffalo from an ex-boyfriend's father, a silver-backed mirror and brush
set from a long-dead aunt, a bottle of cologne purchased in France thirty
years ago. It's the only perfume I've ever bought, which just shows that I
am susceptible to my surroundings, and also that I should make more of
an effort in here. The closet doors aren't closed because they don't slide,
one of them broken some years back. I force my eyes past the bland tangle
of our clothing, the browns and blacks and occasional shout of colour,
the pile of laundry on the floor.

I'm on my bed in the middle of the day like this because I hurt my
back bending over to get a T-shirt out of a box on the floor. I took too
long deciding which shirt to wear, ironically enough to an exercise class,
and my back went into spasm, which felt like a series of spears shooting
through me. I was supposed to teach that night, so a while later I tried
standing, but the spears had left rocks hanging from the vertebrae in my
lower spine. The rocks got heavier and denser the longer I stood. By the
time I reached the bathroom I was eyeing all the hard surfaces my head

would hit when I fainted: toilet, counter, bath. In all the years we've lived in this house, I have never lain on the bathroom floor, which seems emblematic of something: maturity, or just a duller life? What I realized down there was that the feeling of lying on a bathroom floor is pretty much the same no matter the cause: sheer desperation has gotten you there, your head whirls, you may be sick, and you wonder how long you'll be there before someone discovers you.

So many people have written so well about loss, I don't know why I mention it here. Perhaps making it the colour of my bedspread and the mess on my dresser makes it more tangible, and therefore measurable. I've cleaned since, thereby proving something about either the power of words or simple attention. For the first few days after I rose from my bed, every time I got near my dresser, I would hear the lines I wrote about it and be disgusted, so I took a dry cloth and wiped at the dust that had gathered all winter, funnelling up through the vents: dust and cat hairs, bits of ourselves and our stuff flying through air and settling like snow, like judgment: car fumes, insect wings, the mandibles of ants pummelled thin and unrecognizable by air and pressure and specific gravity.

I love that the language of science makes lines that echo out of formulae and of minds that spin vectors out of the air. I spin ant mandibles and think of the line of sticky stuff I've wrapped around the birch tree in our front yard, given to us by a dying friend. A weeping birch, fittingly enough. Though I did not weep when she told me to. "You can cry, you know," she said. I was visiting her for the last time, and I couldn't cry. We were sitting in my car parked by the ocean in Victoria, where she was living in a palliative-care hospital. I had brought new clothes for her, new thin clothes to fit the body that cancer had made of her. We went out for a drive and then to a restaurant that was too loud for the voice she had left, and so it was hard for me to hear what she was telling me—of doctors and tests and finally letting it all go: the fight with chemistry and her cells.

During her last visit to our house, Leah bought us the sapling birch. We admired the curve of the trunk, forced into an S-shape, and we planted it in the centre of a small grassy area next to our front walk. The *S* is still there, thickened, and the branches have extended out so far we have to trim them so we can walk our path. Every spring an odd-looking man appears on our front steps. He has shears in his knapsack, and he tells me that his mother was an arborist, and that he knows that the tree needs pruning, "a proper pruning," he says, casting an acerbic glance at the branches above the walkway that I had just trimmed a few weeks earlier, thinking whenever I did of Leah, and then of haircuts and how I'm not very good at those either. The man makes me follow him down the stairs and under the tree so I can see what he's talking about. At the time of year he comes the tree is full of aphids, and ants crawl up and down the trunk. "It's getting sick," he tells me. "It needs more air."

When Leah bought us the tree, my husband said, "She knows what she's doing." I may have been upset then. He may have been trying to calm me down. Before she met him, I'd told Leah I wasn't sure about marrying a saxophone player. "I mean, he's not, I don't know…" and what I meant, because he's going to read this and ask, is that I thought that because he didn't leap at the idea of going out to see foreign films, he wasn't sophisticated and complicated. "You're wrong," Leah told me. He is complicated. Anyone who has a Marci Lipman print on the wall is complicated.

Leah sat in our garden for our son's first birthday, wearing a big, beautiful red hat, and she laughed at our son's smile. If she were here now, she'd still be beautiful, and her hair would still be thick, and if it had gone grey she'd dye it the same rich browny-red that was her natural colour, and she'd sit in our backyard in one of our fake Adirondack chairs, looking cool and pale even in the summer heat, and she would admire my little writing studio and she'd ask the kids intelligent questions that didn't make them want to flutter away. We'd talk about her work. If she was still doing it, or had she opened a studio of her own by that time, had she become the artist she always was? Her photos were full of her intelligence, and even though they were of oil executives and derricks and pipes and cranes, they were also infused with her warmth (it was something in the light), and maybe too, sharp edges, which I miss now. I miss everything. There are people who aren't afraid of being sharp. She would ask probing questions, which I need, and she would be gracious and charming to my husband and he would come out of himself a little, and by that I mean come out from under the heavy mantle of his responsible self, and he would laugh and be the man I had married, the man Leah had helped me see when I was so anxious about this business of forever.

I google Leah's name, hoping someone might have built some kind of internet memorial for her, but it was too long ago. Instead I find others with her name. A woman who bore a daughter and named her Earline. This unfortunately named Earline went by the nickname "Teenie." How they got that from Earline, I can't imagine, though it's not difficult to imagine why she'd want to be called anything else at all. This Leah and her Earline are from New Orleans, so next I think of our trip there last summer and how Leah would have laughed about my falling in love with a drawing of Paloma Picasso by her mother, Françoise Gilot. The drawing is called *The Letter* and it shows Paloma looking, presumably, at her mother with the same marvellous blend of irritation and intelligence that I see in my daughter when I interrupt her. Eighteen thousand dollars. Leah would have enjoyed that conversation, the drawing I nearly bought with the money I don't have.

After the restaurant, Leah and I had sat by the side of the road and talked, and we might have held hands, and she might have told me about saying goodbye to her family, including the siblings she'd lost touch with. She was content, she said. She had voiced the things she needed to voice. That was when she told me I could cry, and I didn't. Eventually I drove her back to the palliative-care wing and saw her settled into her bed in another of the new tops that I'd brought her, and we hugged goodbye. Later, I phoned. I wanted to tell her that I had been walking past a gallery and had seen a print that made me go still inside. "I bought it in memory of you," I was going to say, because I had finally felt how much I was losing. But she was on to another stage of her dying and had finished with the part I played in her life.

THERENESS

THERE ARE FINCHES in this place. They dart between the trees, flying towards the sun, so I can't tell if their breasts are yellow or just catching light. Yesterday I read about not being bound up by anxiety, and I taught a woman who was caught in it herself. She was stuck, trying to write about her daughter's pet rat, and then after I spoke to her of her fear of writing, I could see the relief on her face, the words spilling out of her and onto the page.

What is it about morning light, the in-betweenness of it, that space between night and day? Just now two crows flying overhead, their wings working the air, the whoosh, whoosh of their work. Feathers and sinew and hollow bone against gravity, a steady muscled beat. Behind all this the hum and blat of engines, a loud burring plane. A bird landing in a maple sets the branch swaying, gold feathers against dark welt of fir mountain, soft chirrup, low in a throat, a round sound. Round.

I spill an entire cup of milk, wipe carefully at the little well of liquid. Will this room smell later, I wonder, but don't really care now. The rain is pelting down on the roof in waves. It has moods, west coast rain, comes in swells, then eases again, a steady falling down of ideas. The other day a poet talked of snowflakes as stars, the heavens shaken, and I thought of a moment years ago in the mountains, when I stared up into the black sky as great pillowy flakes of snow fell out of the darkness, and the cold wet made kisses on my skin.

Tea and morning. Cool air. A mist hanging. Below pillowed in a cleft between mountains and trees. A nest of mist and soft light on the tips of things. I think of a writing exercise a friend described where you're not to use abstractions or the verb "be." "Language is enough of an abstraction," he said. On the internet I find E-Prime, a movement that advocates the abolishment of "to be" because it's imprecise and lends itself to dictatorial pronouncements. This reminds me of times I've said to my husband, "Stop making pronouncements. Say *I*," I tell him, "not *you*." The E-Primers believe that saying one thing is another is "pernicious"—a wonderful word, right there—and go on to suggest that we should all be trained in writing without "be," as a form of "semantic hygiene." To my ear, this sounds like ethnic cleansing for language, but that could just be me, being sensitive. In E-Prime I would have to say "*feeling* sensitive," thereby eliminating any smack of judgment.

"Life is a verb," a fortune cookie tells me. I take the slip of paper out of the cookie and slide it behind the clear plastic sleeve in front of my driver's licence. Now if I am stopped by cops and asked to produce ID, they will see this first, and we can have a conversation about verbs instead of my speeding or other bits of perniciousness.

A breeze sweeps the heat away for a moment. Periods of clarity, then another wave of fatigue sweeps in and takes me down. With mountains it is the pushing up against the wave, the sheer ridiculousness of it, the utter beauty, that need. The "thereness" of them, a friend explains, then doesn't say any more, so I am left with the word, an abstraction to ponder.

In the valley where my father grew up, the mountains cut off the sun in winter and new mountains grew in the streets, splitting the street in two. Men brawled in the bars, the railway ran through then stopped. Snow washed down, sluiced down, sweeping cars, trains, people in its path. My grandfather went to a train wreck to help a man with a broken leg trapped inside a car. The snow swept down, a second avalanche, he and the man hurtled farther down the mountain. They survived, and I wonder what they thought in those moments, hearing the coming wave of snow. Would it rumble like water. Would there be shaking before it hit, would the hit be like a slam or would there be a sweeping up first, being lifted on top of a wave and riding its bubbling surface the way it feels when a wave is an energy field underneath you and you realize how small you are, how powerless, and that the best you can do is to keep your body flat—a plank, so the roiling energy under you doesn't notice, doesn't catch hold and pull you into its torment.

A man walks by. Damn, he sits. Where's he landed from? He reminds me of an old friend, handsome, blundering. I feel he wants me to pay attention to him but I have come to this place to retreat, to not pay attention to others, and so I resent his presence, his mind leaning up against mine.

That morning a finch had hit the glass door next to me, and I watched its slow recovery. It fell, but caught itself on a piece of trim near the bottom of the door, then flew to the wide railing, where it perched, its head dropped to its chest, absolutely still. I worried it would fall again, worried that I should do something for it—intervene somehow, but what would I actually do? I had no idea.

The man asks if there's a restaurant nearby. I tell him I don't know. He smokes. His hair curls. The wind blows. I ignore him. Ignore. Another verb. Requires a greater state of presence, feels more active than giving in and speaking to him. I am in the midst of this ignoring, busy with it, while his smoke blows towards me, and I breathe it in, nicotine air.

When he leaves it's with a little scrape of his chair, a scrape of complaint and resentment.

Days later I take my son to the mountains and we snowshoe on the trails, light mist falling on us, damp air, the snow in the trees building weight. Every once in a while, a slight shush as a clump cracks away from its branch—a seam opening, then the separation and the silent fall, then the whump as it meets the ground. We learn to recognize the initial creaking split, to listen for and feel the drops of heavy water that precede a fall, the wind shaking liquid from the branches, a warning spray—we run on our shoes, our big flat duck feet paddling over the snow.

BIRDS

Beauty can save the world.
—Dostoyevsky

A MAN USED TO sit on the mailbox at Commercial and Charles, a curving shape above the hard metal rectangle, dark against light. His hair fell in lank curtains over his face, his spine curved forward, legs folded under him like a bird's. It could be startling, the sudden shape, dark, looming above. What if he was suddenly inspired to leap? There'd be those bones, that long thin body falling.

Perhaps the man had always sat high above things. Perhaps as a child there was a tree where he could perch, or the roof of a house. One day I noticed him at the same time as I saw a woman walking towards me smiling and talking loudly. I thought she was talking to the man—that she'd recognized him and was greeting him as an old friend. Her face was puffy and corrugated with acne scars. She was missing her two front teeth and her hair hung alongside her face, like his. She leaned forward as she walked, as though into a wind. "I don't know where I am," she said. "I don't know where I am." She sounded happy about this not knowing, as if she'd wakened into a new world, surprising and wonderful, as if she could start again.

Sometimes you look in. Sometimes you look out. When you do there are a thousand things at once. One day it was wheelchairs. A man in a chair on a walkway far from the road, surrounded by empty space. I asked if he needed help. He said no, he was waiting for a bus. An hour later, another chair, this one on a side street, the empty chair facing me, and a man on the ground in front of it. I thought he had no legs at all, and might be in trouble, but when I got close I saw an army blanket under him and a solitary leg. The man was stretching, and he was bent so far forward he looked like a piece of paper folded in half. He looked up as I approached. "Do you get charley horses?" he said as if we'd been having a conversation all our lives and were picking up where we'd left off. "There's a spot right by your left baby toe that releases them." He had an open face, wide-spaced, almond-shaped eyes, a scruffy thin beard and moustache, long uncombed black hair. His voice was full of airy notes. Behind him another man nodded at me as he passed behind the chair and went into a doorway, so I knew my concern wasn't necessary. I wanted to leave but not desperately. Perhaps this man was used to people interfering with him, motivated by do-gooded-ness or pity or what? The folding man kept talking kindly to me, he was filling up the space where I could have been embarrassed by the gaffe I'd made.

I go to a pub in Gastown to meet some younger friends. The friends talk about their lives, and I'm half listening, admiring the room, the ceilings high, the windows long and deep. It's dark out, but the streetlights cast a yellowish glow. A figure passes. Because of the light, she's more of a silhouette than a full shape. She's bent forward almost ninety degrees at the waist, her elbows held up behind her and hands bent, maybe for balance. Her arms look like the wings of a small bird when it's newly born, and the feathers are still wet and clinging. But she isn't wet. It's a nice night, relatively speaking. She walks in a jolting gait, a slight fall forward with each step because there is something wrong in her hips or her knees that prevents smoothness or grace. It isn't right to say there was no grace. There was a beauty in her and a terrible strangeness that I don't know how to explain. The shape of her stunned me, like a blow. I don't know why. I feel her pass as if she's walked across my heart, which sounds melodramatic, and maybe it is. Beauty makes us stop, but is it always "beauty," or is there some other word for it?

John O'Donohue said, "The wonder of the Beautiful is its ability to surprise us. With swift, sheer grace, it is like a divine breath that blows the heart open. Our joy in the beautiful is as native to us as our breath. A lyrical act where we surrender but to awaken."

At home I look up "phenomenology" and get caught up in a talk on YouTube by the philosopher Alan Roberts. I like his voice. I like the way he begins his talk by using a cartoon, the "Numskulls from Beano," then explains that phenomenology is about the things we notice. He writes on a flip chart, listing the layers of consciousness. At one point he says something ordinary, but it's a concept I try to teach, so I write it down, playing the video back a few times to make sure I get the words right. It's a simple idea, and at that moment it seems necessary and profound. "We bring subjects under umbrellas so we are actually making things simpler, gathering information and seeing commonalities between them ... so that you have to remember less and less and yet still understanding more and more."

For a long time I've been thinking about how much people like to count and organize things. I've never been good at it. I get lost thinking of the places where things intersect or the murky in-between states where things are not one thing or another, but sometimes both. Roberts talks of an ordering in Samkhya philosophy, the highest level being "purusha," or "pure consciousness," and the lowest, connected with the world in all its gritty, tangible, messy dimensions, as "prakriti." I like these words. I like listening to and reading people who are trying to understand how we think. Parsing thought, like parsing sentences—is it like making lists? Edmund Husserl, the godfather of phenomenology, said we have to suspend ourselves in time, wait for meaning, whether reading a sentence or listening to music. Is this the same as standing in a grocery store lineup?

Suspension: crows on the hydro line outside. One cawing. The other looking about. They're about five feet apart. Below them, the small chairs we gave our neighbour, a grey cat between them. If you are reading this, you are suspending yourself in time, waiting for my meaning to reach you. So am I. Waiting for meaning.

In *Incognito*, a book about perception and the brain, the neuroscientist David Eagleman says our minds make assumptions. We see what we expect to see much of the time. I didn't expect to see the woman bent at ninety degrees. Is that why she was so striking to me? The phenomenologists talk about intention. You have to intend to look before you really see an object; otherwise it's all a sort of haze. In Aikido, Sensei would say to let my eyes stay "soft," meaning not to focus on the attacker (thus be drawn into his or her orbit), but to be aware of the surroundings as well and therefore not be surprised by the knife being pulled from the pocket or the second attacker emerging from behind a tree. I looked outside that night. Was I distracted by the woman's odd, jerking movement, or was I looking for distraction? Or have I so absorbed the Aikido lessons that even when I sit with people in a comfortable pub (albeit on the Downtown Eastside, where bodies have been known to be flung up against glass), my attention is soft, my focus diffuse.

A while ago I stayed in a house that perched on the edge of a cliff above the ocean. I was sitting on a windowseat trying to write, wrestling my mind for an idea, just one, a thought, a path through words, when a small flock of birds flew past. They were flying just above the waves so I could see the tips of their wing feathers curled up at the end like the flaps on airplanes. The birds flew past—four of them, four crows—and I felt the relief of that, the way it cut through and made something clean and clear in my mind.

I read my notes from Roberts and understand none of it. I watch the video and believe as I'm watching that I understand some. But possibly it's my mind drifting off, caught by entrancing ideas, forms in the language that catch on forms in my mind: "The nothing out of which everything comes" and the word that follows, "Purusha." In the bar, the younger people were talking of their lives. Their faces intelligent, unlined, hopeful. I enjoyed them, their friendliness, their openness. It is too simple to say here that the woman outside had once been unlined and possibly open. We can't know that, can only guess at whether she had had a happy childhood, loving parents, before she was struck down by bad health, bad luck, and then beaten further down by our harsh society, which does not love the broken or the unfixable.

The philosophers argue about innate knowledge. Some say we have it, some say not. I find an article that says researchers have discovered collections of neurons that may serve as building blocks, or forms. The word "idea" is based on the Greek word for pattern or form, and so I go back to umbrellas and lists and wonder if I have forms for birds and men in wheelchairs, do I also have a form for women who are bent with the weight of their lives?

METHUSELAH

I have already lost touch with a couple of people I used to be.

—Joan Didion

"O F COURSE I'M GOING TO CLIMB IT," the woman said, looking at me with that "why state the obvious?" question on her face. "I'm here. I have to do it." We were in the cooking shelter at Taylor Meadows campground on Garibaldi Mountain, a starting point for several hikes, including the dramatic Black Tusk, which rises above the mountain like the black tower in the *Lord of the Rings*. We had arrived by hiking three hours up from the road, our packs laden with tents and supplies and at least twenty pounds of food, or so it seemed to me. I was worried that our nineteen-year-old son, who even at that moment looked like he might eat the table, was going to starve. The woman had given us her leftover Kraft dinner, and my husband was cooking chicken he'd insisted on bringing. "It wasn't that heavy," he still protests when I complain. "You weren't carrying it," I remind him. I had asked the woman about the Tusk because we were still considering our options for the next day, and I was curious besides, having admired it so often from the car on the road from Whistler.

"It's not hard," the woman said. "And you're not exposed. You're in a chimney. It's quite safe. There are lots of handholds." "What about the top?" I said, thinking, and you're safe on a ladder too, until you fall. "The top is fine. It's flat, and yes that's exposed, but it's absolutely gorgeous."

She smiled and left, a no-nonsense kind of woman, the kind I try to avoid, myself being full of quite a lot of nonsense.

"Let's go up there," my son said, without hesitation, and I looked at my husband, knowing he would happily have joined him. He is comfortable climbing on our roof to clear the gutters or patch things. He walks up there with confidence, while in the house I listen for his footsteps and wonder if our life insurance is up to date. But he said nothing, and when my daughter and I chose Panorama Ridge, he agreed.

The next day my whole body felt like someone had poured flour in my veins instead of blood. But we were walking through meadows blooming so profusely with wildflowers it looked like someone had cast bouquets through the grass. New vistas opened over every knoll and around every turn, and I felt like we should be yodelling or singing "Edelweiss." I looked at my kids when I could see them, several hundred feet ahead, and my husband, also some distance away and thought of a friend, an athlete, whose teenaged children and younger husband are all bigger and stronger than she is now. "I'm getting to the point where I can't keep up," she told me, looking, for a moment, infinitely sad. I nodded in sympathy. These are the shocks you get in life. Not keeping up. It's inevitable, but that doesn't mean it's not a surprise.

According to the map, the trip from the campground to the top of the ridge is four and a half miles. By the time we reached the base of the ridge proper, I was counting my steps, something I do when I need to stop myself from looking for places to lie down. A man who looked to be as old as Methuselah passed us on his way down the path. He tripped and recovered himself so easily he made it look like a sort of dance. We smiled and said hello, and I continued my laboured upward steps, thinking even Methuselah, who lived to 969 years old, apparently, was fitter than I.

We stopped and ate an orange. I produced chocolate. The next hundred feet I felt almost hopeful again, though the ridge was getting narrower, rockier, higher. Panorama Ridge rises above Garibaldi Lake to a height of almost 7,000 feet; it's 2,000 feet up from the meadows where we had camped. The trail was getting steeper and more diffuse, broken by rock and open to the sky. Our children were a long way ahead. I babbled to my husband about feeling better, as the trail veered right towards the edge, which wasn't, as these things go, all that edgy. If I wanted to fall there, I'd probably have to jump, and then would just roll and roll and roll, and yes, maybe break some bones. This didn't matter. My rational self, possibly overwhelmed by fatigue and whatever's wrong with my circulation, gave out.

A fear of heights is common, according to Wikipedia, and so are fears of "ghosts, evil powers, tunnels, bridges, and cockroaches." I generally don't worry about ghosts or evil powers or tunnels or bridges, and the cockroaches that inhabited our house when we first moved in didn't disturb me that much, even the one that crawled out from behind the faucet when I was in the tub, but I've been afraid of heights as long as I can remember. My mother had this fear, my siblings do too. Fear is one of the innate emotions. Joy, sadness, and anger are others. How odd, really, to consider emotion. Part of the survival apparatus, but really, just odd.

On the ridge the fear seemed to come from deep in my body like a wave that was going to sweep me up and toss me over the ridge. I felt woozy and a little sick, my mind swimming in some kind of electrified fog and my body uncertain. I wasn't surprised, had already warned my family I might not go to the top. At a place where the ridge levelled out and the rock and dirt gave way to snow, I told my husband, "You guys go ahead. I'll wait here."

"You okay?" he said. "I'm fine. Take your time. Have fun." I smiled, and he shouted up to the kids to tell them to wait for him, then turned to me again. "You could make your way down from here if you like, and we'll meet you at the bottom of the ridge or down by the lake." At the thought of facing the stretch of path I'd just scrambled up, steep and littered with small stones (as treacherous as ball bearings, I thought) and dry dirt, next to an edge where all I could see was sky, I said no and walked over to the opposite side of the ridge with snow on it. We'd been watching people slide down a snowy slope to the left of the ridge. I thought maybe I could cut out the rest of the climb and just slide down from where we were, but I couldn't see the bottom. I imagined jumping just to get it over with. My husband was watching me. I forced myself away from the edge, forced patience, and walked back towards the path. "I'm going to wait here," I told him, and sat on a rock.

People streamed past me. It was as if the whole world had read *Into Thin Air* and wanted to be in a line of people going up. No one even paused, though I could hear fear in some voices. Some, I imagined, thinking as I used to, Why did I agree to this? How much farther and when can I have tea? But they kept going anyway. Why wouldn't I? I did in the past. I was able to manage the phobia then—at least I did for a while. I climbed rock walls and mountains, for a time followed a man who would eventually climb the Eiger and other insanely frightening mountains. When I think back to that time, I wonder what version of myself I was then, or was that a completely different me that's been layered over since, not just with more flesh, but also more fear, more doubt, more anxiety? The day before, I had recognized the name of a mountain on a map and pointed to a peak in the distance across Garibaldi Lake. "I climbed that," I told my family, disappointed when they didn't seem more impressed or even dumbfounded. Me? Climb a peak with ropes and then rappel off the top without bursting into tears? But maybe they just couldn't imagine it, which wasn't that surprising because even as I was pointing it out it felt like a fiction.

There was a gap in the stream of people, then another set of footsteps, another set of lungs panting. The sounds passed me and then stopped. I opened my eyes to see a wobbly-looking older man standing a few feet away. He was dressed in ordinary clothes and had an open, kind-looking face. We smiled at one another, and he waved his pole up towards the snow slope above us, the one I couldn't look at for fear of seeing someone slide off it. "I'm following my daughter," he said. And then asked why I'd stopped. "I'm terrified of heights," I said, feeling for a moment how freeing confession can be, letting a piece of truth slip out without the usual modifiers to ward off shame or embarrassment.

The man nodded. "I don't really do this kind of thing." He pointed up the mountain again. "It's my daughter." I nodded too, thinking of my daughter, who I'd abandoned to the mountain and the care of her father and brother. I wondered how she was doing. I knew she was nervous, but determined. Her boyfriend had been there just a week earlier with friends. She had already done a lot of hiking and was strong and sensible, so I wasn't that worried, but still felt I'd failed her by showing myself as weak and lesser-than. The man and I talked about the weather, and where we were from. I liked his company. I could tell he was as reluctant as I was to be up there. But he girded himself again and faced the mountain, a better parent than I. I watched him begin to ascend the snow slope, but not for long. It made me dizzy to turn my head and the fear rose again as I imagined him sliding helplessly over the edge.

·

Women are more prone to phobias than men, I learn. As with almost all the bad things. We are more anxious, more depressed, and more phobic than men. Some say it's because of hormones—the ebbs and flows of estrogen and progesterone, which are like tides. The sea sweeping in and out again. Storms, shifting currents. And just when you get a sense of the pattern of it, you recognize the signs, they change. You've entered a new phase. Colette Dowling, author of *Red Hot Mamas, The Cinderella Complex,* and many other books about the female psyche, says that with less estrogen women are doomed to "reduced brain power along with increased levels of anxiety, depression and other mental illnesses." That's not very reassuring. What happened to We are women, hear us roar? I search among scholarly articles in hopes of something to offset this narrow, darkening view. It's not reassuring. Estrogen is important in building dendritic spines, thereby helping to create links between neurons, says one article. Stress hormones increase with aging, says another. This is depressing, my body against me. I picture my mind flooding with bad hormones, my neurons losing contact with one another as the spaces between them turn from ditches to chasms.

We keep our balance by using our eyes, our proprioceptors (sensors on the nerve endings throughout our bodies that tell us where we are in space), and the tiny labyrinth of the inner ear, a delicate system of canals filled with fluid and hairs that helps us maintain equilibrium when we're moving. Tip your head down to the right and the liquid in these channels dips down on one side of your head, up on the other, like a glass. Your eyes, meanwhile, slide the other way, so the image you're looking at remains in the centre of your field of vision. I love this—the body, a delicate and intricate machine.

Unless a person has vestibular damage, acrophobia is considered a learned fear. Therefore it can be unlearned. I know this is true because I've unlearned it before with the climbing, but mastering a phobia is, apparently, not like riding a bike. You have to keep practising. At home, I climb a ladder to do some kind of task and feel it immediately, the dizziness, the mistrust of my own body. It's so physical a sensation it's hard to believe it's just in my head. I hang on to the underside of a door frame or some other small point of contact for balance and this makes me feel so momentarily clever and competent, I'm distracted enough to finish whatever job I'm there to do.

The day I decided to give up climbing I was a few hundred feet up, safely clipped into a bolt in the rock and sitting on a small ledge. I was belaying my partner as he climbed the next pitch above. I looked down, curious to see what death looked like. The fact I wasn't afraid, some kind of miracle.

I had learned by this time that at crucial moments where I might fall if I didn't pay attention, a voice in the back of my head would tell me what to do. This voice was always precise, clear, unassailable. It wasn't God, and it wasn't my mother, though it sounded as clear as both, a sort of God-Mother combination, Charlton Heston and my mother combined. As I looked down, this voice spoke again, and this time it said that if I or my partner made even the slightest error, we could both die. This should have been obvious to me, of course, but the voice was never sarcastic. "This is not your death," it added, speaking for the first time in editorial terms, instead of instructions.

Last spring my husband and I hiked in to the base of the Chief, site of my last climb. We stared up at the wall of clean, beautiful granite, rising higher than we could see without backing up, straining our necks. There were climbers nearby, a couple making their way inside what looked like a corner, the rock split in straight clear lines. They moved slowly, their voices happy-sounding, their lives dependent on their ropes, their chalks and slings and carabiners. I remember some of the language of climbing. I remember the electric feeling of being surrounded by air. On the way there, I had climbed up through the woods, following a route that wasn't really a route but was marked by the occasional impression of someone else's foot on a bit of forest duff, and a bit of moss scraped from a cleft in a boulder. Some of this scrambling approximated climbing. I had the same intoxicating sense of upward movement, only without the fear. And so for a moment I felt what I had given up, it shot through me the way an orgasm does. Did I say that? Oh, what the hell. Say it. And so then I wondered what I had done, walking away from something I must have loved. When I put the question to my husband, he said, "You can't do everything," and while I agreed, and know at some level it's true, I'm still confused between the things I could do if I wanted to, and the things I won't.

My family descended from the ridge, my daughter's eyes wide. "You are so lucky you didn't go up there. You would have freaked." I laughed, glad to be absolved by her, if not by myself, and then followed them down, keeping my focus on the path, on weighting my feet, concentrating on where I placed them.

We had a picnic beside one of the small lakes, and they showed me the pictures they'd taken at the top—the three of them standing with the backdrop of sky and snow, Olivia sitting, her legs hanging over the edge, the brilliant blue of the lake visible far below. She was trying to smile, but looked sick with fear. "Oh dear," I said, recognizing what I have passed on.

RECEPTORS

RETRO TENT

EVERY SUMMER I go camping with a couple of friends and our children. There's the cold lake, the clear sky, the mistakes we make every year. We were camping later than usual this year. It was September. The campground felt different, fewer families, more trucks. And our group was smaller, it was just me and Janet, and my teenaged daughter and her friend, instead of our usual pod of eight.

The first evening Janet and I were sitting by the firepit trying to coax actual flames out of the smoke when we heard footsteps on the gravel next to our cars. We turned to see a man standing beside my car. "I'm just walking on the path to the lake," he said. We watched in stunned silence as he walked right into our campsite, past the cooler and the kayak paddles and the sleeping bag covers that no one had put away yet. In all the years I've been camping no one has ever done that before. Was it because we were women? Was there something in our posture or manner that suggested it was okay that he walk into our space without invitation? He was heading for the narrow space between the picnic table still cluttered with the remains of our dinner and Janet's tent when she called out, "Don't go that way, there are ropes."

"You're going to trip," I added, but he ignored us. He could see perfectly well that the only ropes he might trip over were on the opposite side of the campsite. They belonged to my tent, my husband's 1974 Canadian Tire special with guy wires protruding from every sagging corner and pegs half into the concrete-hard ground. The kids called it the "retro" tent, and they took pictures of it, the thin nylon, the orange walls. I like to use it because when there's a storm, the walls billow in and out around me, and I lie inside, feeling as if I'm inside the wind or a balloon, and it's the whole world, breathing around me.

After the man walked past our half-cleared-up dinner, the salsa bottle, the candles, the plates cleaned and drying on the dishtowel, we continued by the fire, poking and blowing at the coals and talking about the people across the road from us. The very young mother and her very young partner, the trucks they drove, many many trucks it seemed, too many for the number of people there, and the dumbness of them. That was Janet's word for them—"dumb." She's not afraid of straightforward words; whereas I would say, not the sharpest knife, or not very smart, or if I was feeling very frustrated, "idiot." So, you get the picture. Neither of us feeling very generous at that point, not open-minded or kind-hearted or any of the things we'd been raised to be. There was a terrible racket going on in another site. It seemed about thirty people were there all talking at once. Kids mostly, so I tried to build my tolerant mother mind up as I chopped some kindling more finely. But it was loud, a wall of noise that pressed in on us further.

We had the fire going by the time the man came back. This time it was dark, and so he was a shape emerging from the forest, a shape that was darker than the night around us. Janet and I stood up at the same time and walked towards him, a kind of two-headed mother force. Janet said, "Can we help you?" which struck me as brilliant and gracious and amazing all at the same time, because what I had wanted to say was, "What the fuck do you think you're doing?"

Instead, following Janet's lead, I put on my teacher voice, which is what I use to make myself more positive than I actually am. I had my flashlight in my hand, a little four-dollar light I'd bought at the hardware store at the last minute. I pointed it towards the woods beyond our fire and said, "Here, let me show you a really good way to go," immediately regretting the "really" because I could hear the lean I'd put on it, as if it were a leak in the sentence where the anger could get out. But as I walked towards the woods, he followed and Janet moved behind him, and it was as if we were herding him, as we would a squirrel or a chipmunk after our food, rather than a strange man in our territory at night.

I stopped at the edge of our site and pointed my little beam into the woods. "There's a path right over there," I said.

"That's not a path," he argued. "That's the woods." He was right, of course, but I wondered at someone who could say "woods" as if I'd suggested he walk undefended into a jungle thick with hanging vines and snakes instead of an area so thoroughly scavenged by campers looking for burnable twigs its floor was as clear and barren as the floor in a mall. "There's a way through here, see?" I said, pointing again. He muttered something but followed the light. Janet and I looked at one another with relief; then we sat again by our modest fire and talked in the way that grown-up women talk, with all the layers of our lives underneath the conversation, as well as the layers of responsibility we had taken on—for my part—so blindly, so ignorantly. This job of being a parent can be a shock sometimes. You go for long periods driving them places, lying awake waiting for them to come home, trying to ensure they go out of the house with most of their body parts covered up. You're in a muddle but fine, just mildly stressed, but then it hits you that it's entirely on you to keep their giggling oblivious and naïve, and it's not possible, but still you have to try because it's precious and thin and it's the whole world, breathing.

BEAR SIGHTINGS

THE NEXT SUMMER I went on a different camping trip with a different friend but the same two girls. Shortly after we arrived, the campground manager, who looked all of fifteen, wearing a uniform that bagged out from his slender body and a wisp of hair on his upper lip, came to tell us that a bear had been seen just ten minutes earlier in a nearby campsite. He called it a "bear sighting."

"Where?" we asked. "What happened?"

"Site 13, down by the supervisor's site." He stopped, as if he'd said too much, and so my friend asked again, "What happened?"

"Our dog scared it away." The boy's face lit with seriousness as he spoke, and I marvelled at that. I've been watching kids' faces for years and wondering over the way thoughts skitter over them like clouds or maybe windows or paper or sky—and that it's like watching neurons fire. I'm not saying this well. I found this boy beautiful, and I fell in love with him a little. Or maybe it was charm. I fell in charm.

Normally after news like that, I would react with a lot of words and would spend the rest of the day being anxious and picking up crumbs. But I wasn't upset, not the way I usually would be. Maybe it's because I was with another woman, not my husband, who would be so busy pretending that bears didn't matter that I'd have to compensate. That's the thing with couples. You make a unit, so when there's gaps, one of you has to fill the spaces between. My friend and I talked about the basic principles of bear avoidance, and after we cleaned the previous campers' discarded carrots and other bits of garbage out of the firepit, and, yes, okay, after I picked up every crumb from our picnic table, we went to the dock. The girls jumped in the lake and my friend did too, performing a graceful dive off the top of the railing and then striking out into the middle of the lake without looking back. As I watched her swim farther and farther away from us, I pictured the bear making its way out along the rickety planks of the dock to where I sat contemplating the water and my level of interest in getting cold. Would it fall through where the planks were rotten, or would it be so focused on coming out and eating me that it would instinctively pass over any bear-trapping holes? I eased myself into the lake, thinking about swimming bears and wondering if my front crawl would be good enough, or would the bear bypass me and go for the girls, who were playing on a log nearby. Then I made myself stop, recognizing a thought too far. I have rules about my imagination. It's not allowed to hurt the children.

Thoughts are thin beams of electricity and chemicals that shoot out into the space between cells. Experts say that to increase the connections between cells (i.e., to build and strengthen the pathways between neurons), we need to increase or enhance the receptors. So it's the catchers, not the pitchers, that complete a thought. This makes me wonder if my mind is shooting out good ideas all day long, and I'm just letting them fly past without even noticing them.

For the rest of that day I got quite good at stopping myself from thinking, which means that rather than letting the bear thoughts get picked up by their usual receptors—a team so well rehearsed they're like a chorus line—I was diverting them, putting up interference. I was proud of myself for this, walking around almost like a person who was confident, and I congratulated myself for not staying in a state of anxiety over the mere idea of a bear and thus keeping my fear sensors on alert just in case.

A while later a cop car drove past our site, and shortly after that, we saw the boy riding past on his bike, so we called out to him, "What was that? Why are they here?" He stopped his bike and pulled it to the side of the road and told us with the same serious face and the same careful manner that there had been an "incident of domestic violence." Again I admired the way his face shone, and I wondered if his parents had taught him to use that sort of language, and did they speak that way around the dinner table: bear sightings today, waste-removal issues, site 29; or if it was something he'd heard on TV. We asked for more information, and he told us that a woman had been assaulted by her husband. "She's pregnant," he added, and I wondered if an adult would have told us that much, or was he upset and just needing to let the words out. It seemed wrong for someone so young to be dealing with such a dangerous situation. "Is she all right?" Jane asked, and I could tell by the gentleness in her voice that she was also asking, "Are you all right?"

"She's with friends."

"Where's the man?"

"He went off into the woods. There are trails here that lead out to the road. We think he went out there, and that his mother is coming to pick him up."

Jane and I looked at one another, and I know we were thinking the same thought: what if *I* were that mother?

At night the world reverts to prehistory. The shadow of the earth falls on us, and the trees become sentinels, the rocks dark mysterious shapes. That night it rained, so we set up a tarp above our picnic table and burned candles low on the lids of jars, and we laughed, and everyone's face glowed, the rain and the dark around us making a little pod of light.

We all went off to our tents, Jane and I separately, the girls together in theirs. I'm happy enough in tents. It's a little like being a kid again, in a fort or cocoon. Most nights, but especially on camping nights, I have to get up at some point. Always I wish this weren't so, but it is, and so then I lie there awhile and think about the dark and wish there could be a catheter just for camping trips. Then I think about the bear and the angry perpetrator of domestic violence—what if he didn't find his mother and so now he is an angry perpetrator of violence against mothers? Or what if there was some other randomly angry man lurking among the trees waiting for hapless, peeing victims? As well as mad men, I know every bear story there is: the camper in Yellowstone dragged out of her tent in the middle of the night, the Native elder in Lillooet stalked and killed by a black bear. And then there are the aggressive deer in the interior who corner people in their driveways, and the seventy-five-year-old woman at a petting zoo who was felled by a llama, ostensibly because it wanted the grain that she had in her pack, but once she was down some goats climbed on top of her. I think it was a team effort. I think they were celebrating.

In his book about writing, *From Where You Dream*, Robert Olen Butler says "the human condition resides in the details, the sense details," and so when we want to convey emotion on the page we need to focus on the tiny particulars that the mind pins itself to. When I have to go out in the night I'm not thinking of conveying emotion, but controlling it, so I go out into the dark by segmenting it, I look at the spaces my flashlight illuminates, nowhere else; and I trust in my peripheral vision to detect malevolence or wildness outside the thin beam of my light. I keep that down, to the necessary, to the ground in front of me so I won't trip, and I do not scan the area, I do not want the flashlight or my mind to go beyond its narrow scope of attention. I do not want to allow for these other facts to take hold: the potential for lurking murderers, skulking bears, marauding llamas. When I crouch down, I think about my shoes and not about my back exposed to the night. All of these thoughts are constructions: neurons and receptors, pitchers and catchers, carefully maintained bits of chemistry and light.

The next day the boy came around at noon after we were supposed to be gone and asked politely if we had decided to stay another night, and we said no, we were going soon, and that we'd be quick. He said, "The campground's full," and he didn't say anything more. He didn't seem to know how to say, "Please leave now because you're supposed to be gone already, and I may need this site soon." In his restrained silence, my friend said, "We'll be welcoming if we see anyone looking." I thanked him for taking good care of us, and we said goodbye but carried on with our plans, which were to stay longer to swim, to let the girls kayak a little. I felt guilty about transgressing, not just against rules, but against the boy's innocence. Sure we were nice people, or so we painted ourselves with our couldn't-be-nicer smiles and greetings, but still we cared more about our plans than the rules he was paid to enforce, and so we'd betrayed his empathy and innocence. I imagine him next time he's faced with anxious campers, thinking of us, the women he'd reassured with details, who'd acted just like everyone else in the end. And I hope he'll stay strong, though I worry he won't. Because how can innocence survive when even the grey-haired mothers exhibit perfidy and decay?

LANYARD

WHEN I GAVE A writing workshop at an engineering firm downtown last year, someone gave me a lanyard with a guest card hanging from it. I love wearing a lanyard. As soon as I hang it around my neck I feel more sure of myself, as if the little emblem of belonging is evidence of some larger process of vetting and assessing, and I've passed the test.

In this case the lanyard was simply to allow me access to the bathroom, which was outside the locked doors. I've never been good with keys, and I'm not any better with cards. I hold them too long or not long enough, and then I don't give the machine time to recover before trying again, so things jam up, and then I'm refused entry. I stand outside these doors (usually glass) looking helpless and flustered, which no doubt undoes much of the work I've done to make me look like I belong there.

When I work at places with lanyards, I put on makeup and fuss with my hair. I wear pants that I bought from Superstore (Joe Fresh, $39.99) in a steely corporate-looking grey. They go with the jacket I bought from Value Village and the top from Costco. I am a fraud, obviously, because people who work downtown surely do not shop at box stores and Value Village, and the women do not imagine they can get away with the flat-heeled boots that I wear—expensive, but three years old and scuffed—sensible boots, because who really wants to walk in heels, and what is the point of that at my age? Never mind my age. When I consider heels, my mind flips into hippie mode again, which is never far from the surface, and I want to deliver a polemic on the socio-political, not to mention medical, implications of wearing them, and then I wonder why that particular self and not some of the more useful selves—say those developed in the last twenty years—aren't more immediately accessible. The other day at a conference the speaker used the line "these aren't my people," which has become something of a catchphrase, or at least that's how it caught my mind, the "my people" business, smacking of high school and being "in" or "cool" or whatever, but I knew exactly what he meant and I knew the moment when I had finally felt myself belonging, and how good that had felt.

When I teach a group of people I've never met before, I'm nervous. I know they will be curious about me. They'll be considering my clothes, my hair, my face, the way I carry myself, the way I speak, and at some level they'll be deciding whether or not I can do anything for them—while I'll be considering whether to turn and run.

When you teach you have to maintain an upbeat tone and manner. You have to locate a voice that is appropriate for the job. I think of this as acting because I don't think this voice is really mine—it's confident, attached to a person who can stand in front of a room full of people she doesn't know and pretend it's fun to be there. This is a search, an experiment, a high-wire dance. I didn't know I had this voice in me until a few weeks into my first teaching job when I realized that even as I was buying the cup of tea before the class, I was already standing straighter and looking the cashier in the eye as I offered up some cheery word or quip along with my change.

I teach voice in a creative writing class—and I make a joke of it, as in "How do I get one?" And then we look at various writers with their various voices and marvel over the myriad ways that personality can come through words.

On CBC one day, I heard the English writer John Lanchester say he thinks the idea of the "stability and continuity of the self" is exaggerated, and he believes more in the Buddhist idea that there's a "succession of selves," and that our feeling of being fixed is a "trick of memory." I love this.

A succession of selves. That makes sense when I look back at earlier phases of my life and find it hard to recognize the person in them. I also think we develop a set of selves (or personas or voices) for each of the everyday roles we play: teacher self, writer self, mother self, wife self, friend self. Is it a trick of memory when I walk into a classroom and start with a smile, so everyone thinks I'm happy to be there, or is it a bit of cataloguing acumen—knowing where to look for the appropriate self?

In his essay "On the Necessity of Turning Oneself into a Character," Phillip Lopate says this:

> It is an observable fact that most people don't like themselves, in spite of being, for the most part, decent enough human beings—certainly not war criminals—and in spite of the many self-help books urging us to befriend and think positively about ourselves. Why this self-dislike should be so prevalent is a matter that would require the best sociological and psychoanalytic minds to elucidate; all I can say, from my vantage point as a teacher and anthologist of the personal essay, is that the odor of self-disgust mars many performances in this genre and keeps many would-be practitioners from developing into full-fledged professionals. They exhibit a form of stuttering, of never being able to get past the initial superficial self-presentation and diving into the wreck of one's personality with gusto.

When Lopate talks about the "wreck of one's personality" and "gusto," I fall a little in love, and later in the same piece when he speaks of "the need to go beyond the self's quandaries to bring back news of the larger world," I cheer. In another piece he says something about using the self but going deeper in, and I think of Joe Simpson's terrifying and riveting book, *Touching the Void*, about falling into a crevasse and having to go deeper into the cleft in the glacier to rescue himself. This idea, not of climbing up and out but going further in, makes me squirm.

I have a feeling the engineers aren't interested in voice and wrecks and gusto, though I'm pretty sure they care as much as I do about belonging. In a couple of the sessions I've taught I had a sense that I was walking into a kind of club, a fairly happy coterie of people who were doing work they loved with people they either respected or enjoyed making fun of. Before one of these sessions, I was even offered a beer. I probably should have taken it. It might have loosened me up and made my lesson on grammar helpful instead of soporific. "Grammar is a piano I play by ear," Joan Didion said, which I'm not sure the engineers would have appreciated. It's important, I'm sure I told them. But if I'd said that a sentence is a pipe; it needs to convey something ephemeral but clear and certain as glass—or oil, maybe I would have done better. Or maybe it would have been too obvious. The word "teacher" carries so much baggage with it—the idea that the person at the front of the room knows more than the people in it, for instance— an impossible load to carry.

I taught business writing about five times. Some of it was fun. Some of it reminded me of being on a mountain with nothing but my fingers and the tips of my boots holding me to the earth.

Belonging is about finding the right voice inside yourself, I decide, or maybe it's knowing your own voice when you hear it. I decided to stop teaching business writing last year, not because I thought it would kill me but because I realized that my pretend business-pants-and-lanyard-wearing self was too thin. I haven't inhabited that self fully. She's not infused with belief, and I think what I mean by that is that she's not infused with my real self, which must be the self that loves what she's teaching so much that she can forget she's afraid of standing in front of people. This may be part of getting older, this paring down, the sorting and rejection of the not selves—a growing pile. It's not that I have anything against engineers and business people. It's that I don't sufficiently understand what they do, and so I'm in thin air when I stand in front of them, a wide-open empty, lonely place. "Follow your bliss," Joseph Campbell famously said. My bliss is a tangle of voice and word and language and mystery. It's deep inside a sort of crevasse, the walls are dark and warm, and I have so much to learn there.

TWIN SET

ANXIETY AND DEPRESSION, like a twin set, follow me some days. A haunting, not an entire possession. In middle age it seems they've settled on cheap couches in the back of my brain and colonized from there, rewiring whole segments of thought, setting up undercurrents throughout so every activity has a fear attached, a what-if, a thread.

When I was a kid, my cousin and I spent an entire morning inside a story that centred around a spider web between two shrubs outside our grandmother's cottage. The web interfered with the path to the door, but we decided that it was necessary and had to be preserved. We made up an elaborate story that involved a lot of stepping over and going around one of the shrubs to do it again. I don't remember anything about the story, just how deeply we fell inside of it, this world we'd made. My uncle came out to see what we were doing and because he liked to fall into stories too, he joined us in stepping over the web, and then it became a thing all three of us did, long after the web was gone.

I was happy then. Most of the time I'm pretty happy now, but sometimes it feels as if I've got a trip wire in my brain, like the web, and that if I forget to step over, I fall inside a different sort of story, one full of anxieties and doubts and nasty little tangles of fear. This story takes place in a room that looks like a public toilet, the kind you find in the Toronto subway, all cold tile with sound bouncing from the walls and the metal stalls that have locks that stick or are broken off entirely. There's an attendant. Her head lifts as I enter, and she studies me glumly. I am meant to do something for this attendant, but I'm not sure what. She stands between me and the towel dispenser, which is empty. She watches me expectantly. She knows I'm going to screw this up no matter what I do—offer a coin, it won't be enough, a friendly word, it'll be the wrong word or the inflection will be off—as it usually is, she will be quick to point out. I've never understood social interaction. I'm a failed interacter. That's been clear from the start, she reminds me.

I glance away from her quickly, go into a stall and attend to my business there, aware that every sound I make, the time it takes to reassemble my clothing, is being totted up against me, my poor taste in general, my inability to recognize quality or to pay for it evident by the way the zipper catches, and the button hangs loosely by its cheap thread. I wash, mentally reviewing the state of my skin, any open wounds for germs to burrow into? And try not to think of the invisible, the insidious, definitely not cleaned off by the attendant, who is slumped on the floor now, the few muscles she has weakened by the very sight of me, my inadequacies one too many burdens for her to hold, so her legs fold up under her.

On bad days, the attendant is accompanied by the depression chorus. The chorus is a set of weedy-looking creatures, something like teenagers who have been eating too much pizza and watching *Criminal Minds* for too long. Their hair is lank and greasy. They have piercings in questionable places and they maintain a fixed expression of disdain and contempt as they hold their towels high and move together like Leonard Cohen's backup singers: Cohen's singers if he didn't pay them and they weren't in love with him, or were angry because he was paying attention to someone else, and they've watched one too many times as his body got all loose and comfortable around this someone. They've sneered as he took off his hat. They've hissed at that whole sex monk god thing that he has going. There's a smugness in the depression chorus, along with huge slatherings of bitterness, high-pitched and off-key. The chorus hums faster and faster like in the nightmare I had as a kid where my parents would find me walking up and down the stairs, which were starting to melt in my dream, the molecules of the sturdy beige broadloom devolving, pooling, as if heated, into a sort of stew.

This all sounds quite terrible, I know, and I don't mean to depress you. I'm not depressed as I write this. It's just a thing to write about.

Those days come, and then they go again, and then sometimes on the other side of them I hear a joke or make one, or else I just decide to hell with it. I'm done here, and so I get up off the couch and make some tea and call a friend and there I am again.

I went to see Leonard a few years ago in Vancouver. He was well into his seventies by then, working to make back the money his manager had stolen from him. You would think that stealing from Leonard would bring such a doom upon you and all your progeny, an enormous cosmic curse, that you wouldn't dare, but I suppose this person had his reason. Leonard was magic. At the beginning of every song, he'd walk to the front of the stage and kneel on one knee, then rise up smoothly, and you would see the control in that and think of the years he'd spent on his knees learning to be human. (I'm still trying.) I would try not to think of my own knees as he did this but to admire his humility instead. Then he'd go over and stand next to the mandolin player so we could see that he was some kind of magician, playing precise, tumbling cascades of notes. Later he would do the same with his backup singers, so we'd hear how clear their voices were, pure as bells.

I'm happy now, thinking of Leonard and trying to find a word that means angelic but isn't. The depression chorus is on the couch, smoking and watching TV and chewing gum and drinking all at the same time. They like to keep busy when they don't have me to bother. They watch reality TV so they can pick up new ideas for snide remarks and they check each other's nails and look for nits in their hair. I let them be. It's not good to pay them too much attention. I know they're there. The webs they make slip through my thoughts like whispers.

ANKLES

My daughter is graduating from grade 12 this year, an event requiring photographs and dresses, two so far. To my surprise, she agreed to go shopping with me. We went to several stores. There were dresses she couldn't look at because they were too much like dresses her friends already had. Then they were too long or too shiny or too . . . We went to so many stores, I said, "Why don't you go look on your own? You can always bring something home and then take it back if you change your mind." I came home from work a few days later to find a dress draped over the banister. Stretchy beige T-shirt dress with a lace overlay, a modest scoop neck and long sleeves. I told her I thought it looked nice, asked if she'd model it for me, but she was busy, a soccer practice, friends coming over, something. Days passed. Maybe a week. Eventually she put it on. Maybe it was the light. "Whoa," I said. Her face fell. "Well. It's pretty. I mean. I like it, but don't you think it's a little small?"

When my mother was born, women were still wearing dresses that came to a point well below the knee, revealing their ankles and not much more. I wonder if it's my mother's sensibility objecting, or if I have just morphed into a prude, the usual story—wild youth, censorious middle age.

There's a discussion. We go shopping and she tries on the next size up. It wrinkles oddly around her waist. I bring her a black one, which doesn't seem so skin-tight somehow, the colour pulling light in. A man standing in the hall next to us is waiting for his wife. He doesn't seem to be looking at my daughter, but because he could, I want to scrape his eyes out.

While this is going on, a friend helping me research another essay is sending me articles about atrocities against women. I read these stories with horror. I imagine stalking about our streets, then going to other countries and yelling at men. Instead I stay home and tell my daughter she can't wear the tight dress. This is backwards. Or frontwards. I don't know. I nearly burst into tears later that day when friends ask me if I'm okay. No. I'm not. Not okay. I think I should be stronger, clearer, more certain of the lines that are drawn, I imagine, everywhere. Lines that other people can see, that make life simple, direct, the boundaries certain. When I tell my husband about the dress debate, he says, "I would have just said, not that one. Move on," and I think, right, of course, and I don't tell him how aware I am of where she is in her life. Seventeen, humming. The body blooms. There is a bloom. Do we bury it under heavy cloth or do we celebrate? Do we tell her she should hide herself, deny this bloom? Or do we let her learn to negotiate within it?

In Egypt women are protesting and then being dragged through the streets and beaten and imprisoned. Then they go home and are beaten by their families, by their brothers and fathers. In India, women are groped, beaten, raped and burned. Female fetuses are aborted there and in China. In North America women are splayed out on billboards, admired, stalked, harassed, abused, raped, beaten, murdered.

I go to buy a new bra and am shocked by the pumped-up contraptions hanging on the wall, bras with gel packs inside them, so you can buy yourself a pair of breasts and strap them on. Then you can buy booty packs to stuff in your underwear so your bum looks big. I thought we didn't want big bums? "I can't keep up," I tell my daughter. She laughs. She likes it when I admit ignorance. "I could buy a dress that's cut down to here," my daughter says, pointing to her navel. "And slit up to here," I say, pointing to the top of my thigh.

In the *Globe*, Margaret Wente writes another of her inflammatory articles, this one about how women have to protect themselves from men because men "always want sex more than women do." She cites some study where women went out and asked men if they wanted sex. All the men said yes. When the men went out and asked women, the women said no. Really. Did the study consider control? As in another version of the experiment, or did they consider the simple factor of power and strength? Most women are physically weaker than most men. As in, we can be overcome by sheer strength. I am reminded of that sometimes just standing next to a man. I'm vulnerable in an elemental way, and there's very little I can do about it.

I buy my daughter the dress. I have already helped her select the shoes. Five-inch heels. This is akin to binding her feet, I tell her and her friend, who has just shown me a picture of the shoes she'll wear—five-inch platforms that look like something out of a cartoon. "That's what my mother said," the friend says, her voice light, her eyes clear. They have just been to a talk by Roméo Dallaire. He spoke about rape camps in Rwanda. Is it wrong that I am glad that he has saved me, the mother, from having to say "rape"? When I was sixteen my mother walked me to the bus stop one night. We lived in a valley. The road up was narrow and twisty and dark. There were a lot of trees, the houses set back, few street lights. "I just want you to be safe," she said when I asked why she was doing this. "What about you?" I asked, "when you walk back down the hill alone?" I was by that point four inches taller than my mother. She was slight, grey-haired, and if an attacker couldn't see the way she was piercing him with her eyes, he probably wouldn't know to be scared of her.

My daughter's friends come over to our house to dress before the photo. They come down the stairs on their shoe stilts. No one falls. I am in our hallway when they come through. They tower over me. It's like being suddenly surrounded by a flock of very large birds. They flutter, they giggle. They pose for pictures, and then I watch them totter down our stairs. I worry for their ankles.

TRUST

"JUST STAY OUT OF MY LIFE," my son said. He was seventeen, standing in my office looking down at me, not yelling, though it might have been better if he had. I sat helpless and dumb in my chair. I might have said okay or why or nothing at all. He might have answered. I don't remember. I remember feeling as if I'd been stabbed, and that I didn't blame him for saying it. I knew I'd caused it by rousing him out of bed two mornings in a row, not yelling, but haranguing, walking into his room, opening the blind and turning on the light and saying, "What are you doing? How do you expect to do anything in your life if this is your attitude? You can't get into university like this. What's going on?"

I'm not sure exactly what had driven me to change my habit of letting him make his way to school (usually on time) at his own pace. It might have been because I'd been listening to other parents and wondering suddenly if I was too slack. Some of the worst mistakes I've made have come from thinking I needed to impose the lives of other people on our own. That's one theory. The other is that every once in a while my mother marches through my veins. Her commands clear as a bell sounding, or a bugle.

When our kids were young, Barbara Coloroso's popular book on parenting was going around the neighbourhood. Coloroso categorizes parenting styles as "brick wall" or "jellyfish" and says that if you grew up with the brick wall you were likely to be a jellyfish, and vice versa, and that you should instead be a "backbone" parent. I saw her point. But that didn't matter. I have done exactly as she predicted, swung wildly between styles—one day jelly, the next brick. My children seem to have survived, but on bad days, when I'm doubting myself, I sometimes wonder what damage I have done. And sometimes I think the damage is to me.

My son is nineteen now. He's moved out. A month before he left, I went to a presentation at the school called "Building Bridges." The room was almost empty when I arrived, a subterranean room in the school with concrete block walls, utilitarian chairs and tables. As I walked in, my shoes echoing on the hard floor, I was thinking I was about four years too late. There were just a few people there. One of the presenters came over to me right away and introduced herself. I liked that she had a streak of blue in her hair. "Could you sign the sheet and then make yourself a name tag, please?" she said, then turned to greet someone else. I walked towards a table near the front of the room, while the teenager part of myself argued that I should go to the back, where I might be able to walk out if it got weird.

A short while later a man sat next to me. He was a little older, like me, I suppose, but very trim and neat. He pulled out the chair next to mine and sat. We chatted idly at first—How old? How many?—in the way that parents do, and then he said something about obedience. That it was important. I answered in a noncommittal way, hoping that if I didn't outwardly disagree, we could just move on to another subject and then I could stop feeling so anxious. Some time ago I read that we have brain cells throughout our bodies—in our spines, our stomachs, our knees. The brain cells in the back of my knees were jabbing at me. It was all I could do to stop myself from running out of the room.

After a little introduction, the instructor asked us to tell the person next to us one good thing about our child. "Hard-working," the man said right away. I could see he was sincere, love and pride beaming from him. I took my time coming out with something, and he misunderstood, thinking I was having trouble thinking of a positive trait. I said, "It's hard to choose just one attribute." "I know," he said, "I could go on and on," and then we smiled at one another, united in loving our children. "Socially adept," I said finally, which made him pause, and I realized I'd done what my father would do, use too many syllables for something simple. I used to think he was showing off. Now I realize he was just struggling, as I do, to find the right word, while some nerdy gremlin from an unused part of my brain pipes up with the longest word it can think of, which is not, most of the time, socially acceptable behaviour. It's as bad as correcting people's grammar when they're talking. It's as bad as a lot of other things too. But never mind.

The instructors wrote down the words people called out: "intelligent, funny, athletic, kind, thoughtful, helpful." And then they said that they liked to do this because most parents when they get together tend to complain about their children, so it was good to remind ourselves of their positive qualities too. We all nodded, and I wondered what sort of dramas these women had seen. I thought they looked well able to manage them. They struck me as the kind of people who knew that the best way to meet most problems was kindness and an open mind, and maybe they didn't have to struggle to do that. Then I thought about how obnoxious it would be if everyone went around bragging about their children all day and how alone that would make me feel, especially if I'd had a bad day and was lost inside that other stew, the one where my child has told me to butt out and where I feel awful for making him feel that way. "The best thing I ever did for my daughter," one mother told me long ago, "was to trust her." I've remembered that, partly because I like the woman so much, and partly because it made sense to me. The gift of trust. I didn't know at the time how hard that would be.

"I have not stopped being a teenager," I tell a friend the next day, and we laugh as she tells me that now if she's flipping out about something, it's her son who is the mature one. "His voice gets softer," she says. "He's the psychologist now." We consider the possibility that it's not our children rebelling, but us. Some nights lying in bed waiting for our daughter to call, wondering where she is and not able to sleep because we don't know, I say to my husband, "I don't actually want to be doing this anymore"— meaning I want to go to sleep and try to live my life instead of worrying about someone else's. My husband agrees. And then one of us gets a glass of wine, while the other picks up the cell phone again and stares at the screen. "Anything?" Neither of us can sleep in these circumstances. For my part it's because my heart has blown up like a balloon inside my chest and it's aching. It's hurting like hell.

During the workshop the woman with the blue streak in her hair explained about brain development and all the changes the human body and mind go through from thirteen to eighteen, and again, I thought, I'm too late. Why did I wait so long to do this? I think she said, "It's like they're crazed, or they're in a fog. They're not really conscious of you at all. There's so much going on with them. They're growing intellectually, emotionally, physically. They're trying to figure out who they are." This made me feel better, somewhat. I thought of my son scuttling down the basement stairs to get away from me and I thought of my mother, and the way she used to follow me around asking questions, and how I never understood how inadequate she felt until now.

I just phoned my son. He's been home for dinner on the weekends. I've seen his place. He's not that far away, but he's not here. And when people ask, and I say, he's moved out, a part of me doesn't want to answer, doesn't want to touch that hole there, that ache where the wind goes through. We talked a little. It was fine, I told myself, but not fine too. Sometimes I have to struggle for things to say. Sometime long ago, it seems we lost the ability to talk to one another, or maybe it was never really there. I don't know. I'm the mother. I'm supposed to know. When he was a baby I used to wonder what he would talk about when he grew. For a while, as a toddler, he would talk so much sometimes—about a lamp, about the diggers in the street, what were they doing, and why and why and why. I'd think, tiredly, okay, let's be quiet for a while now. And then later, when he became quiet, as a teen, when he tunnelled into his lair in the basement and didn't want to talk, I lamented every bad mood I'd ever had, every quiet moment of my own. On the phone we are polite. I hear in his voice that he wants to go back to his life. I hang up, missing the sound of his feet on the stairs, the different quality to his tread, light and heavy at the same time.

Some of the cells from the fetus stay with the mother after a pregnancy, apparently. Scientists have found them in the brains of dead mothers. Does it help to know that my children have left bits of themselves inside of me? Does this make me feel less alone? "Go for the lightness," my therapist says, and I think, am I dead? Dead mother walking. I remember being inside a cave, the black so deep and rich and velvety, my headlamp so feeble and small. The lightness my therapist refers to is possibility, hope, trust. People always say, Let them come to you, etc., but they don't understand emptiness. It's hollow and it stings, like when you get smacked by a ball and you're winded. Is this how the rest of my life will be? An ache where my son was? He's not that far away, but I've been missing him for years, missing that little boy who'd come running to me, who'd hold his arms up to me to be picked up, the baby I rocked, sang to.

I know people who do this properly. They're braver. They're stronger. I wilt. And then I think this is exactly why I shouldn't have had children.

I'm not strong enough for the job. Last summer I went for a picnic with two other families. It was devastating. The other families seemed so perfect and complete, all their children with them. My daughter came. My son went and played street hockey with his friends. Street hockey is code for smoking pot, I say to my son, and he protests wildly. "It is not! We play!" These picnicking friends are fabulously good people. They're what I would call "straight" when I was younger and smoking pot myself. I watched them interacting confidently with their children, demanding attention, being bossy, loving, but authoritative, strong and certain. My daughter seems confident and certain too, and I have no idea where she got it from, unless it's because we were less tense with her, less worried. I'm still too worried. My son looks back at me sometimes, clear eyed, intelligent, observant, healthy, and I think, what am I worrying about?

One time when I was visiting my mother in the home, I said, "Thank, you, you were a good mum" to her. She was teary. This is what kills me now. My mother was never teary. "I was too bossy," she said. "No you weren't," I told her, though she was. "She's going to have us cleaning the place with toothbrushes if we don't find something to do," one of my friends had said on a day when we were lounging about, dangerously in my mother's mind, I'm sure, or just getting on her nerves. My mother may have been worried that because we were all there, the son of one of our family friends and three or four others, she was responsible and should be making us do something wholesome and pure, not sloping about the place, sidling up to one another, humming with hormones and barely suppressed lust.

My mother's been gone a long time, and I still miss her, but now my children are teens, I recognize her in myself: the way I freeze sometimes, feeling shut out and hurt and not knowing what to say, then pressing too hard, asking too many questions or the wrong questions, not being calm and secure in myself, as I should be, as the woman with blue hair seemed to be at the front of the classroom, as most people seem, even the ones in that room full of adults who had all shown up, presumably because they also felt like they were failing, or were like me—slammed open by this, the shock of feeling our children pulling away from us. So often when my kids were young and I was tired and I had no moments for myself during the day, I longed and grieved for the self who could sit and think a thought from one end to the other. So, I was grieving then. I'm grieving now. Even then, when my son matured a little, moved from one stage to the other, I would miss the old stage, the just sitting up stage or the just learning to walk stage, that look of absolute pride and delight on his face as he tottled between us.

"Take care of yourself," the instructor said at the workshop and showed a slide with an airplane safety image, the mother with the oxygen mask already on helping her young child beside her.

"Can I say something?" a woman asked from the back of the room. "There are times when you just can't do that, take care of yourself, that is, or all hell will break loose. So I'm sorry, but whenever I see that thing, I think, not that again."

The night our son told us he was moving, I told myself, it's fine, I'm ready for this, it's meant to happen, while another part of me felt my heart split in two and fall dead to the floor. So I thought, fine, I can live like this, heartless. Then I took a step and tripped. There was my heart, attached with long strings, two shards of myself banging about my ankles.

After we talked a while, and our son went downstairs to his room, I went to my husband. I was already crying. He held his arms open to me as I sunk into his chest. "It's beautiful," he said. "Aren't we lucky to be going through this?" I wanted to hit him, but cried instead.

"Now you have to get on with your life," my therapist said, and I thought what a shelter it's been, hiding behind motherhood. What do I do with all this bright, stinging air?

I drove my son over to his place for his first night there. He showed me his room. It's painted a ghastly blue, as in bright and insulting to the eyes. It's about one-third of the size of the room he has at home. His sister's twin bed with the drawers underneath fits next to the small desk beside it. He has a bookcase and a closet, and that's it. A room. The rest of the house is fine, nice enough. I walked around, complimenting it. I hugged him and said goodnight. I went home, focusing on the fact that he'd taken me to see it, that he wanted to show it off. He's not leaving me, I tell my heart, which still dangles on its strings, wavering in the space he's left behind. He's starting himself.

EVERYTHING RUSTLES

IT'S 5:30 IN THE MORNING, a few hours away from sunrise. I'm outside stoking the wood-fired boiler at my brother's place on Gabriola Island when a sudden beam of light pins me to the boiler. Or so it seems. As if I were a butterfly on display, stabbed between the shoulder blades. Why does it seem that would be the place? It just does. Hard white light, slamming me against metal. I turn and see headlights at about 100 feet. Aiming straight at me. I stare at them, expecting them to swing, back away. I'm thinking the car must be heading for the ferry, and it's people who've just realized they've forgotten something and are turning around to go home and get it. I move out of the path of the lights to a shrub near the boiler and watch the lights. They don't move, and then they go off.

I hear nothing—the crackle of wood in the boiler, my breathing, the fan whirring—nothing. For a moment I'm still rational, still in my managing mode, the mode that got me out of bed that morning—my last morning here—feeling happy, thinking of the useful practical things I would do before leaving. I consider walking up the driveway to see what's going on, but it's a long driveway. My brother's place is on five acres, and the small spill of light from the house doesn't even reach me at the boiler, thirty feet away. I've left the flashlight inside. I imagine myself halfway up the driveway and fully surrounded by dark and emptiness in the tunnel of trees, with all those black shapes and the rustle of small animals in the brush. A thread of fear unfurls inside of me and makes my breath go shallow, my heart race.

As I head towards the house I regret every mystery novel I've ever read, every TV thriller, every scary movie. In all of them it's a woman. She's alone and she's doomed. It doesn't matter that by instinct and luck I have weathered some situations. I have read *In Cold Blood*. I know what happens to people in isolated places in the dark. I go in the house and close the door behind me. It's a glass door. The murderers/rapists will see me at the same time as I'll see them. We'll lock eyes through the glass, and they'll see that it's all over but for the killing. I turn the deadbolt and go to my nephew's room, where there are blinds I can peer through, but his desk is up against the window and I need to be close. I go to the laundry room instead, where my brother has installed machines that look like they've been designed by NASA, as if laundry were a serious venture. Maybe it is. Maybe I missed the memo. The window is long and deep and looks out on the driveway. I lean against the wall, the lights off. I can see where my sister-in-law parks her van, and past that to the rock at the centre of their turnaround, the shrubs growing around it, and beyond them, the empty driveway, the dark forest.

It's early December, that time of year when everyone is in a low-level panic, and the dark seems to go on forever. All week I have been sitting in front of a different window on the other side of the house, watching light and trying not to. Why go to a beautiful place when you want to concentrate? What was I thinking? In the late afternoon, the sun would pull its light back in, and there would be patterns across the sea and shadows in the seams between the mountains. In the morning, light seemed to spread like a melon opening, a slow mystery, an unfolding.

As I stare at the rocks on the driveway, hoping to see light growing on them, I imagine what it will feel like to hear footsteps approaching. I imagine my heart scuttling up into my throat for protection. I imagine myself simply floating up into the air, the cells inside of me like dead fish floating on the surface of the big bag of water that I am.

"The more you feel fear, the more your brain has the capacity to feel it," I read somewhere. It's like anything you exercise: your abdominals, your math skills. Our minds aren't that different from the rest of us. They get better at things with use, and they get flabby and lazy with disuse. "I will show you fear in a handful of dust," T.S. Eliot wrote in "The Waste Land." "To him who is in fear everything rustles," said Sophocles. I find these quotes later, when I'm safe and rational at home. In the laundry room, I'm not thinking of beautiful writing, I'm thinking of the Westerns I watched as a kid where the good guys holed up in the house while the bad guys gathered outside with guns. How could anyone bear that level of anticipation? I wonder, and I'm serious. If someone gave me a gun, I think I might just shoot myself to get over the suspense.

I stare out the window for at least another ten minutes. A part of me aware that imagining Hoss Cartwright as my saviour is a sign I've been alone too long. The driveway remains grey and silent. Fear needs information to sustain it, I'll read later on. It's anxiety that can run away with you. I go into the kitchen and make oatmeal. It's still dark. The windows are still black expanses all around me. Malevolence could still be outside, but I push the thought away and look up "sunrise" on the computer to find out what time it will be. The sun will rise at 7:56 a.m., I read. Actual sunrise is the time "at which the leading limb of the Sun first rises above the horizon." Limb, I discover, is an official term. I think of scientists who get to name things, who give the sun a limb and are still taken seriously. I imagine a sun with an elbow poking up over the edge of the horizon, a stretching sun, a running sun, a dancing sun.

My oatmeal is ready. I place a chair facing east and sit with the bowl in my lap. Beyond the verandah, the light is coming; the sea, from a distance, looks like a flat plate. There are dark amorphous shadows on it and a boat making a line in a single pale streak of sea. Beyond it the mountains and above them a tangerine seam opening; then shades of grey and light. A crow calls. The trees, slender boles with feathery tops, stand like sentinels. Between them the dark clings while the sky and sea fade to the day's ordinariness, and the land around my brother's house reveals itself in its broad and innocent emptiness.

On my way out, I pass the neighbour's driveway, see how close its entrance is to my brother's, and see a car parked halfway along it. I go home. I tell friends. I'm shocked by how frightened I was. It was a minor incident, a non-event, and each time I relay the story I am conscious of revealing my own anxiety more than of telling people something that will titillate their fear centres. Still, many of the women I tell nod their heads in recognition. "You went outside in the dark alone?" my sister-in-law says, and I feel a rush of gratitude because she acknowledged my fear. "It never goes away, does it?" my friend Jean says. "It's that awful feeling you get at night when you hear footsteps behind you."

But some of the people I tell look at me askance, and I feel a flicker of shame as if I'm revealing something too personal, or I'm showing myself to be nervous, skittish, flighty—qualities I've always disdained. I think of all that time I spent when I was younger dealing with this very fear—I studied Aikido for years. What happened to all that? Where did my confidence go?

When I tell my friend Luanne about the experience, she looks at me with her intelligence, and I have that feeling again, not pinned exactly, but exposed. As if I'm being seen without my coverings, the chimera I've built over the years. Luanne is my friend. I know she's not trying to threaten me. But that doesn't matter. I feel it anyway. I tell her I think it's related to an experience in a campground years ago. She shakes her head no. "I think this is something about your brother," she says.

"No, no. It's not about my brother," I say, though as I do, I think, *maybe*. Was I so afraid of wrecking his beautiful house that I created a fantasy of a bogeyman to distract me? Or was I afraid of the writing I was trying to do? "When we fear things I think that we wish for them ... every fear hides a wish," said David Mamet.

I tell a therapist about the incident, my over-the-top, outside-of-all-rational-thinking fear. She says: "You were afraid because you went into the house. You acted scared, so you were scared." I consider the moment when I decided not to confront the headlights and remember how that had felt like a minor defeat at the time, but I still want to argue, what if there had been a car full of yobs, intent on some kind of mischief?

A friend sends me a list of her fears. It's long. Some make me smile: "When I was little I was afraid of the bogeyman under my bed, some unknown devil who would grab me by the ankles and haul me down to hell. I was afraid of the bears that I feared lived in the front little porch area off my parents' bedroom." But it's awful too: "Now I'm afraid of being attacked by a man—raped and/or murdered. Since I know it can happen. I didn't really believe it until it happened to me."

"Do one thing every day that scares you," Eleanor Roosevelt's famous quote exhorts me from a poster on the wall at Lululemon, where I'm waiting for my daughter to try on some overpriced shorts.

"I'm embarrassed," I say to my daughter, and I'm not talking about the shorts. "I think everybody is," she says. "You feel childish when you're scared." After I get over the shock of her mature response, I say, "I guess we think we're always supposed to be in control, at least I do."

"And then we find out we're not."

I think of the wisdom of the young and then of intersections, those moments when my view of the world goes *skewiff* somehow and I realize I have to readjust my thinking. Carl Jung said that midlife is the time when we need to become who we truly are, rather than who we were socialized to be. If we do this right, he says—in much better language—we won't be so pissed off when we die. I like this sort of thinking. It's hard, though, to look back and not get stuck, and it's even harder to look at where I am, and not think, how did I end up like this?

A couple of years earlier when I'd been arguing with my son over his curfew, foolishly trying to answer his repeated "But why?" I said something about the streets being dangerous at night. I was thinking of a friend whose son had been beaten up, just because, as he was standing waiting for the bus one night. I didn't want to tell him, but I wanted him to be aware, to be careful, to be safe. "I don't want to be afraid all the time," he said. "I don't want to live my life in fear."

I used to be braver when I was young—or seemed to be. I hitchhiked, climbed mountains, skied steep hills, and, for a brief time in the seventies, lived by myself in a truck with no lock on the door. Now I'm older, it seems that fear has moved in. It leers and pulls at me from around every corner, behind every thought, reminding me that decisions have consequences. Accidents and bad luck happen. Evil exists. I think of little old women cowering alone behind their curtains, peering out at the world. Is that where I'm headed?

"Your amygdala has been damaged," the therapist tell me. "It's overactive." I wonder how she knows this as I sit across from her, slumping in my chair, shoulders hunched as though expecting blows. I imagine my amygdala all pumped up, too full of itself, as if it has been going to the gym all these years while the rest of my brain has been lying around smoking pot and watching bad TV.

At home, I read and read. I find out that people who love risk are more sensitive to dopamine, or is it less? And that's why they like bigger scares? I find out that the rush of adrenaline dissipates fairly quickly after a fright, but the cortisol lingers, making us fuzzy-headed and stupid. And I find out that the message from the amygdala to the prefrontal cortex travels a path as clear as a freeway, while the return pathway that reason travels is narrow and twisty, like a country road with sheep lying on it.

You can have a predisposition to anxiety, apparently. A study done with light and minor shocks and images showed that the people who recovered more quickly from the rude treatment were more likely to have a larger structure in the brain near the amygdala. This structure, the ventromedial prefrontal cortex, inhibits the activity of the amygdala, but for people who suffer from post-traumatic stress and those of us with more garden-variety anxiety (i.e., those who fuss over what they said to their neighbour three days earlier over the dahlias), the structure is too thin or too small, and so every time the amygdala gets even a little excited, the barrage of messages saying *Danger! Danger! Run! Hide! Do something! Quick!* doesn't stop.

I'm looking for excuses, I know. It's not my fault. It's my brain structure, my hormones, my overindulged imagination. I study a photo of my mother that I stuck on our fridge a while after she died. She's wearing a toque, knit from multiple neon-bright colours, which sits up high on her head, her grey hair sticking out underneath. We all made fun of that toque, but she didn't care. She's on a ski hill with a walkie-talkie in her hand. A laugh has taken her over, and she's inside of it.

Is this a non sequitur—or an image of how I want to be?

Months later, a friend offers me her place for a week when she and her husband are away. I hesitate, thinking of my fear of being alone and isolated, and mention it to another friend, who says, "You know a woman was murdered near there in the woods."

"I know," I say, wondering if she's telling me because she wants to warn—or scare—me, or if she's giving me more material for my essay.

My friend's place has a large patio with a big glass door. Light spills through it. The house is stucco and clematis grows across the front of it in long, sweeping strands that remind me of a grapevine. I buy flowers and put them out on the patio so it feels like I'm somewhere in the Mediterranean, and this makes me happy, but there are a lot of doors in the house, and every time I lock one, a tiny finger of fear shows me how old it is, reminds me how alone I am, how vulnerable.

I call up a friend who survived a brutal rape when she was younger, and then she survived the trial, which in the seventies was another sort of assault. We talk about martial arts. Elaine studied karate for five years.

"But I'm still scared," she said. "Nothing has changed. It's scary out there. The threat of violence is there, even when the actual violence isn't." The certainty in her voice surprises me. I was expecting her to sound nervous, like I am. This is bracing, like a slap or cold water. I feel something in me waking up. And wonder if I'm two people, one who is afraid and one who is angry.

Elaine continues: "I hate it in movies where some guy is getting beaten and the woman stands there screaming helplessly with her hands over her mouth. I think, why don't you help your guy, kick the attacker or gouge out his eyeballs. "Though," she says, pausing a moment, "I wonder if I could do that, gouge eyeballs that is."

"But if it was your life or his?"

The martial arts, though long in the past, still help us be more aware, we agree. We look around us; we keep one part of our minds attuned to the periphery, to be ready for surprises from anywhere. If she feels vulnerable now, Elaine says, "I try not to look like a victim. I bring my arms out from my body as I'm walking as if I have big muscles. I try to look like, don't mess with me. It's all part of karate. I think about the reaction, to block, punch, kick . . . Yes, I have lots of rage. But you know. You keep your mouth shut."

I hang up, thinking of rage and silence, the veneers we place over our dangerous selves. I look for Aikido videos on YouTube, where I find my old Sensei from Japan. I smile watching him move in cyberspace, remember his chuckling laugh and the grip of his fingers on my wrist, sharp as snakebite.

I practice *Tai-no-tenkan* in the hallway, a deceptively simple step and a turn that we did at the beginning of every practice to warm up, to centre ourselves. "It's in your hips," Sensei would say. "Your *hara*. Your power is there," and he'd point to the place where the ties of his *hakama* joined in front of his belly button. I think of my *hara* and pivot on the smooth floor, thinking the way I used to, of holding myself low and powerful and balanced and ready for anything.

Before I go for a walk, I close the blinds even though it's still daylight because my friend had asked me to, and I see how my mind wants to inject something fearful into the moment—a strange car swinging into the driveway, a figure on the other side of the glass—and I dismiss them, recognizing how much I seem to like scaring myself.

I walk a path through the woods out to Fraser River. The land on the far shore is open, the view filled with light and space. I'm happy out there. Maybe beauty is another kind of awakening. In time, my body and mind swing into rhythm, my torso lengthens, and I feel the health and strength of my body, everything in concert, everything flowing in a rhythm bigger than I am, as if I've clicked into some sort of current that's always out there, and that as long as I'm walking inside of it, I am invincible.